saguaro
the desert giant

Anna Humphreys
Susan Lowell

Rio Nuevo Publishers
Tucson, Arizona

Rio Nuevo Publishers
An imprint of Treasure Chest Books
P.O. Box 5250
Tucson, Arizona 85703-0250
(520) 623-9558

Excerpt from "Saguaros Above Tucson"
  © May Swenson. Used with permission
  of the Literary Estate of May Swenson
Illustrations © various sources as listed on p. 59

Editor: Sarah Trotta
Production supervision: Ronald J. Foreman
Designer: William Benoit, Simpson & Convent
Map: Kevin Kibsey

front cover:
  Cabeza Prieta National Wildlife Refuge, Arizona JACK DYKINGA
back cover:
  Brittlebush and sunburned saguaro,
  Organ Pipe Cactus National Monument, Arizona CARR CLIFTON
title page:
  Sonoran Desert National Monument, Arizona JACK DYKINGA
table of contents:
  Ajo Range, Organ Pipe Cactus National Monument, Arizona CARR CLIFTON

Library of Congress Cataloging-in-Publication Data
Humphreys, Anna.
  Saguaro: the desert giant / Anna Humphreys, Susan Lowell.
  p. cm.
  ISBN 1-887896-30-9
1. Saguaro—Sonoran Desert. I. Lowell, Susan, 1950- II. Title.
QK495.C11 H86 2002
583'.56—dc21   2001005878

Printed in Korea
10 9 8 7 6 5 4 3 2 1

CONTENTS

NEVADA

Lake Mead

HUALAPAI

ARIZONA

Santa Fe

Colorado River

Lake Mohave

NEW MEXICO

CALIFORNIA

Needles

MOHAVE

YAVAPAI

Los Angeles

HALCHIDHOMA

Wickenburg

Roosevelt Lake

Indio

Blythe

1

Phoenix

2

Globe

Salton Sea

COCOPA

PIMA

WESTERN APACHE

San Diego

QUECHAN

Gila River

3

4

UNITED STATES
MEXICO

Gila Bend

Safford

Mexicali

Yuma

MARICOPA

5

6

7

Río Grande

Ajo

9

TOHONO
O'ODHAM

13

CHIRICAHUA
APACHE

Ensenada

8

11

12

UNITED STATES
MEXICO

El Golfo

10

Sasabe

Tucson

Puerto Peñasco

Nogales

San Felipe

Río de la Concepción

OPATA

Magdalena

CHIHUAHUA

PACIFIC

PIMA

SONORA

OCEAN

15

Hermosillo

Chihuahua

ISLA ANGEL
DE LA GUARDA

14

SERI

ISLA
TIBURÓN

Río Sonora

YAQUI

BAJA
CALIFORNIA

16

Río Yaqui

Alvaro
Obregón

Guaymas

Santa Rosalía

Ciudad Obregón

MAYO

The Sonoran Desert
GOOD PLACES TO SEE SAGUAROS

1. Wickenburg-Congress-Aguila Loop
2. Apache Trail
3. Sonoran Desert National Monument
4. Casa Grande Ruins National Monument
5. Ironwood Forest National Monument
6. Picacho Peak State Park
7. Pinal Pioneer Parkway
8. Parque Nacional el Pinacate
9. Organ Pipe Cactus National Monument
10. Tohono O'odham Indian Reservation
11. Saguaro National Park (West Unit)
    Arizona-Sonora Desert Museum
12. Saguaro National Park (East Unit)
13. Sabino Canyon Recreation Area
    Coronado National Forest
14. Seri country, north of Kino Bay
15. Central rural Sonora
16. Area near San Carlos Bay, north of Guaymas

BAJA
CALIFORNIA
SUR

GULF
OF
CALIFORNIA

SINALOA

La Paz

Culiacán

San José del Cabo

From the Hualapais in the north to the Mayos in the south, at least fourteen indigenous cultures utilized the saguaro.

1

The Story of Saguaros

The giant cactus, or saguaro, is the symbol of the American Southwest. Statuesque yet grotesque, this big geometric succulent is the image that springs to mind when most people hear the word "cactus." Like other celebrities, the saguaro (pronounced "sa-WAH-ro") has often been mythologized and often misunderstood.

It's a plant that bristles with personality. Whether standing solo or gathered in a crowd, the saguaro seems to be an oddly human tree. To the writer Edward Abbey saguaros were "planted people."

Saguaros are probably the most memorable features of the wild, vivid landscape of the Sonoran Desert, although they inhabit only part of it. What's wrong with this picture? *A movie camera pans across the majesty of Monument Valley, taking in the stark red cliffs and the bright blue skies. Across the valley, shots ring out and men on horses race after each other. As they tear toward the camera, they pass a tall saguaro cactus, standing alone, silent, wise . . . and literally out of place.*

"The saguaro is a noble vegetable," said longtime Arizonan Glenton Sykes (left), photographed with his brother, Gilbert, at Agua Caliente, near Tucson, March 25, 1908, by their father, Godfrey, a researcher at the Carnegie Desert Laboratory. For the picture Glenton stood on a hidden ladder.

In fact, such a plant could not possibly witness a chase through southern Utah because saguaros do not grow farther north than central Arizona. (Exposed to the bitter winters of Monument Valley, a real saguaro would quickly become a cactus ice cube.) The total range of the saguaro includes about a third of the state of Arizona, a few sites near the Colorado River in California, and about half of the Mexican state of Sonora, which lies immediately south of Arizona.

For at least ten thousand years, human travelers in these arid lands have looked up at the giant cactus and marveled, with good reason. The saguaro is a sight to be seen, an amazing shape-changer throughout its long life, a botanical phenomenon, the centerpiece of the desert ecosystem, and a source of food, drink, shelter, and spiritual sustenance to desert peoples.

Balduin Möllhausen, a German traveler who encountered the saguaro in the early 1850s, proclaimed it "the queen of the cactus tribe." He saw it as "a remarkable tree that had branches but no leaves."

"One of the most remarkable plants on the globe," agreed Carl Lumholtz, a well-traveled Norwegian ethnologist who came across the saguaro in 1909.

"No, no!" exclaimed an early visitor to Saguaro National Monument (now Park), as he contemplated a cactus forest. "It cannot be true! It must be the tequila I had in Nogales!"

The saguaro tickles the imagination. It has inspired paintings, photographs, sculpture, cartoons, and a never-ending stream of curios ranging from lollipops to inflatable beach toys. It is the subject of a shelf full of books, serious as well as funny.

When she came to Arizona, the modern American poet May Swenson first found saguaros "fuzzy and huggable." Then she had second thoughts:

> Each prickly person,
> droll, gregarious, we would embrace, but up close, rigid
> as cast plaster, spikey, bristling—how dare we touch?

Just like people, saguaros stand upright and have arms, trunks, spines, and ribs. As babies, they need nurses to survive. They rise up in generations, they are counted in censuses, and they can be adopted.

Over many decades, even centuries, each one slowly grows into a unique individual, some becoming tall and stately while others turn into tragic, comic, or monstrous figures.

Good times make them fat, and bad times leave them

(l. to r.) Senita, cardón, and saguaro cacti, Sonora, Mexico   DAVID BURCKHALTER

skinny, scarred, sunburned, sick . . . but nevertheless, through thick and thin, more often than not they manage to endure. When the end finally comes, only a skeleton remains. And, maybe, a few old boots.

In a nutshell, the saguaro is the largest cactus native to the United States, often reaching a height of 50 feet, a girth of 2½ feet, and a weight of 80 pounds per foot. Twelve to thirty vertical ribs support its bulk and give it the appearance of a fluted green column set with gray spines. Adapted to drought but intolerant of cold, it nevertheless grows farther north than any of its columnar cactus relatives, which include the multi-trunked organ pipe, the hairy senita, and the hulking cardón. When Saguaro National Monument was designated in 1933 near Tucson, Arizona, the saguaro became the first cactus ever to be protected in a national preserve. Its large white blossom is the state flower of Arizona, although as Edward Abbey pointed out, like all cactus flowers, "it is unpluckable and nearly unapproachable except by an insect." A healthy, lucky saguaro cactus may live as long as two hundred years.

To the earliest Americans the saguaro was something delicious, useful, intoxicating, and holy, and it remains significant in southwestern Native American culture. Later arrivals in the New World have recorded a wide variety of responses, ranging from scientific to hostile. They have also recorded many different names for the giant cactus.

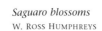

Saguaro blossoms
W. ROSS HUMPHREYS

FIRST GLIMPSE

On their fateful expedition in search of the Seven Cities of Gold in 1540, the Spanish explorer Francisco Vázquez de Coronado and his army of *conquistadores* were probably the first Europeans to encounter saguaros. The records for the expedition, which crossed the Sonoran Desert between 1540 and 1542, show that the chronicler, Pedro de Castañeda, did mention a giant cactus, but he called it a *pitahaya* (peet-AY-yah). This term, used in old Spanish writing (as it is in Spanish today), refers to several kinds of large cacti, so it is hard to tell if the ones Coronado encountered were actually saguaros. Some scholars are convinced by the Sonoran location that they must have been. The Spaniards also observed the native people drinking wine fermented from the fruit of this cactus, as well as making jam and other products.

The plant frequently appears under the name *pitahaya* (sometimes spelled *pitaya*) in later historical accounts. Father Eusebio Francisco Kino, a Jesuit missionary to what is now Sonora and Arizona from 1687 until he died in 1711, noted that the Indians even neglected their livestock in order to harvest the highly perishable saguaro fruit. While doing military reconnaissance from Fort Leavenworth to San Diego during the Mexican War, U.S. Lieutenant (later Major and General) W.H. Emory "discovered" the cactus growing along the Gila River in what then was Mexico and now is central Arizona. He wrote that Native Americans traded cactus syrup for beads and cloth.

As one of the surveyors of the new boundary between Mexico and the United States in 1848, the pioneering botanist George Engelmann christened the tall plant *Cereus giganteus* (SEER-ee-us gi-GAN-tee-us). Engelmann classified the saguaro as a twig on the *Cereus* branch of the cactus family tree, a group of flowering plants officially known as Cactaceae. Using the customary scientific Latin of his era he described the new species in his official report as "*erectus, elatus, cylindricus, cande-labriformis*" [upright, puffed up, cylindrical, candelabrum-shaped], with "*seminibus numeroissimis in pulpa saccharina*" [very numerous seeds in sweet pulp].

Reverting to English, Engelmann observed that the cactus possessed a pericarp, or skin, "of the hardness of a green cucumber" and its flesh was "bitter, and not acidulous," while "the crimson-colored sweet but rather insipid pulp [of the fruit] has the consistency of a fresh fig." He also noted a regional common name: "The *Suwarrow* or *Saguaro* of the natives."

NAMING A CACTUS

Writing a few years later, after the Gadsden purchase required a new boundary survey, Boundary Commissioner John Russell Bartlett referred affectionately to *Cereus giganteus* as "our friend the *petahaya* or Giant Cereus."

The word "saguaro" appears to be a Spanish interpretation of a word in the Cahita language, still spoken by the Yaqui and the Mayo people, who live in what is now Sonora, at the southern part of the saguaro range. These groups probably would have been the first ones the Spaniards asked about the strange tall cactus. At least a dozen variant names found their way into print as the

Cereus giganteus, *on Bill Williams Fork, 1858* BALDUIN MÖLLHAUSEN

PLANTS' RIGHTS

Under the Arizona Native Plant Law, the saguaro cactus is listed as a "salvage-restricted protected native plant." This statement means that these cacti are considered vulnerable to damage by theft or vandalism and are protected by law. Rare cristate or crested saguaros are classified as "highly safeguarded," and even stricter regulations apply to them.

Saguaros cannot be legally removed from any land, including public lands, without a permit from the Arizona Department of Agriculture, as well as the permission of the landowner, whether that owner is a private citizen or a government agency. Any owner of land where saguaros are "growing wild," which means "without being propagated or cultivated by human beings," has the right to destroy or remove these native plants. A landowner also has the right to sell the saguaros or give them away. However, depending on the acreage involved, the landowner must file a notice with the Arizona Department of Agriculture twenty to sixty days prior to removal of the cactus. Saguaros, like all protected native plants, may not be legally possessed, taken, or transported from their growing site without a permit from the same department. Besides the permit, each plant must also be issued an official seal.

Suspected saguaro poachers, traffickers, or vandals should be reported to the appropriate local law enforcement agency, which will notify Department of Agriculture investigators. In Arizona, criminal charges including Class 4, Class 5, or Class 6 felonies may result. Transporting saguaros illegally across state lines is a federal crime under the Lacey Act of 1900 and may result in fines of up to $100,000.

For further information about protected plants, including regulations and application forms for permits, contact one of the Arizona Department of Agriculture district offices around the state, or the web site at http://www.agriculture. state.az.us/PSD/nativeplants.htm.

(above) Roadside veterans, Route 84 near Stanfield, Arizona, 10/26/85 MARK KLETT

(opposite) Saguaros on desert bajada, Sand Tank Mountains, Barry M. Goldwater Range, Arizona JACK DYKINGA

nineteenth century progressed into the twentieth. Which would endure?

sugarro	suaharo	zuwarrow	suaro
saguara	suguaro	zawara	sahuaro
suwarrow	suwarro	sahnaro	saguaro

Eventually, the last two survived—"sahuaro" is closer to a phonetic English spelling, while "saguaro," which now dominates, is perhaps a more correct Spanish spelling. But the wordplay continues.

"We call the ones with hanging-down arms 'SAG-uaros,'" chuckled Melanie Florez, a ranger at Saguaro National Park. "And we call the tall thin ones with no arms 'CIG-arros.'"

PROTECTING SAGUAROS

Not all observers have found the big cactus endearing. In the early 1880s Lt. John Bigelow, Jr., riding "on the bloody trail of Geronimo," descended the Rincon Mountains and crossed what is now Saguaro National Park East. "In the foot-slopes we passed through an ardent grove of giant cacti, called by the Mexicans 'Sahuaros,' some of them fifty feet high," he wrote later. "Among these prickly horrors grew a variety of lesser ones . . ." Unfortunately, the humanoid columnar cacti may be seen as foes rather than friends, as monsters, as easy victims, or as convenient targets. Early travelers described saguaros pierced by arrows, and even Lumholtz collected the erroneous impression that "water may be obtained by making holes in a sahuaro, for instance, by a pistol shot."

Today saguaros are fully protected in several public parks and monuments, and largely so by state law elsewhere in California and Arizona. In Arizona, the plant may neither be damaged nor collected on public land, while a state agricultural permit is required to move a saguaro for sale even from private land, at the risk of a $10,000 fine; nor may saguaros be transported across state lines without a permit. Cactus rustlers are caught on a regular basis. Even so, the plants remain vulnerable to vandals and thieves, although the single greatest threat to their existence is probably loss of habitat to human development. But sometimes even plants have their own means of retribution. For example, as saguaros grow larger and more valuable, they become much less likely to survive transplant shock.

STUDYING SAGUAROS

On the positive side, a sense of personal connection between people and saguaros may help to explain why the giant cactus is the most intensively studied organism in the Sonoran Desert. Much important research dates from 1904, when the Desert Laboratory was established

on Tumamoc Hill in Tucson, Arizona. Like hundreds of public libraries across the United States, this famous center for the scientific study of the desert was funded by the steel mogul Andrew Carnegie.

Since then, Desert Laboratory scientists have unraveled many cactus mysteries, although many more remain to be solved. And besides sponsoring studies of the saguaro's fascinating anatomy and physiology, Andrew Carnegie— probably unwittingly—played another role in the story of the giant cactus. In 1920 two great Carnegie-funded "cactologists" (as they called themselves, and the term has stuck) named N. L. Britton and J. N. Rose published a massive book entitled *The Cactaceae: Descriptions and Illustrations of the Plants of the Cactus Family.* In it they reclassified *Cereus giganteus*, and they gave it a new name: *Carnegiea gigantea* (car-neh-GEE-uh gi-GAN-tee-uh). "It is dedicated to Andrew Carnegie (1835-1919), distinguished philanthropist and patron of science," they wrote.

Some botanists have disagreed with Britton and Rose's classification and retain the original name, but as the Arizona poet Richard Shelton pointed out, where names are concerned, the more the merrier.

"When I want to be particularly scientific and impressive," wrote Shelton in his memoir *Going Back to Bisbee*, "I refer to the saguaro as either Serious Giant (*Cereus giganteus*) or Public Library Giant (*Carnegiea gigantea*), since both names are used by specialists to identify it."

To specialists, however, the idea of having a personal, emotional relationship with the saguaro is wrongheaded.

"More amazing perhaps than any aspect of its biology is man's emotional involvement with the saguaro— the saguaro is a 'hero' among plants," observed Warren F. Steenbergh and Charles Lowe, whose three-volume *Ecology of the Saguaro* (published in 1976, 1977, and 1983) is the most comprehensive scientific study of the great cactus so far.

"Man has endowed it with human attributes and bestowed upon it affection and concern for its 'problems,'" they remarked. But, they cautioned, this may lead to mistaken belief in "myths, half-truths, and . . . sensational and emotionally appealing 'doomsday stories.'"

Is the saguaro a dying hero? Is it doomed to extinction? Not at all, concluded Steenbergh and Lowe after decades of research. Instead the plant seems to be actively evolving, and in the process it demonstrates "a fascinating scheme for survival" in a tough and changeable environment.

Flower, seeds and fruit of saguaro, 1857
GEORGE ENGELMANN

View from Maricopa Mountain near the Rio Gila, *1855* HENRY CHEEVER PRATT

SAGUARO FAQS

Where do they grow? *Only in the Sonoran Desert of southwestern and south-central Arizona and western Sonora, with a very few in southern California.*

How tall do they grow? *Record height: 78 feet. Average mature height: 18 to 30 feet, but often reach heights of 50 to 60 feet.*

How much do they weigh? *About 80 pounds per foot.*

How fast do they grow? *Very slowly, depending on location and age of plant; in general, about 3 feet in thirty years—perhaps a half-inch a year. Growth of one-tenth of an inch in the first year is not uncommon.*

When do they grow arms? *At about 12 feet in height, or forty to eighty years of age. Some never grow arms.*

What are they mostly made of? *Water.*

Can you drink the water inside a saguaro? *No. The sap is slimy, bad tasting, and nearly impossible to extract.*

How long do they live? *Probably up to two hundred years.*

What are the greatest threats to saguaros? *Freezing weather, loss of habitat, destruction of nurse plants, bacterial disease, "browning," old age, lightning, wind, fire, animals, birds, insects, human beings.*

Are they endangered? *Not at the moment.*

What are the spines? *Leaves modified into special needle-like structures that guard and insulate a cactus.*

When do saguaros bloom? *Mostly in April, May and June, from late afternoon to early morning.*

How many seeds can a saguaro produce in a lifetime? *Forty million.*

How many of these will grow up? *Perhaps one.*

Why is that saguaro cheeping? *Woodpeckers and flickers drill out nesting cavities inside saguaro trunks. Later these holes may be occupied by many other birds and animals.*

Dawn, Cabeza Prieta National Wildlife Refuge, Arizona RANDY PRENTICE

2

A Little Cactology

A saguaro is a classic example of a cactus, but what exactly is a cactus? Any plump, prickly, leafless desert plant? Not necessarily. Although cacti are succulents, not all succulents are cacti. Nor do all cacti live in deserts. The word "cactus" doesn't even mean "cactus," technically, since it comes from the Greek *kaktos*, or "thistle."

Saguaros are "something purely and wonderfully American," proclaimed the naturalist Paul Griswold Howes, and he was right. With one exception, all cacti are native to the New World, though they have been transplanted elsewhere. They grow naturally from British Columbia throughout North America (in all but five of the United States) and down to the tip of South America. Certain cacti, including saguaros, can flourish from sea level to a mile high. Still, these spiky succulents like warm climates best, especially the deserts that border the tropics, as the Sonoran Desert does. Like many other plants in the area, the saguaro is basically a tropical species trying to move north.

Not much is known about the progenitors of modern cacti, primarily because soft plants do not fossilize well in dry places. The earliest record of cactus in the southwestern United States dates back only about forty thousand years, a wink in geologic time. Cactus experts estimate that North American cacti originated as small tropical trees near the equator around sixty-seven million years ago, soon after the dinosaurs disappeared and mammals, birds, and most flowering plants were established.

Gilded flicker mates
TOM VEZO

To this day a cactus possesses the same basic parts of any flowering plant—stems, roots, flowers, seeds, and some form of leaf. Many, but not all, cacti have spines in place of leaves, thick stems, and other adaptations to dry climates, yet some species have never strayed from the humid tropics.

Saguaros have, however. Botanists place *Carnegiea gigantea* in its current range at about the same time that the first humans arrived in what is now the Southwest. "This species was present in the Puerto Blanco Mountains of southwestern Arizona 10,500 years ago and in the Hornaday Mountains, Sonora, 9,400 years ago," noted Raymond Turner, Janice Bowers, and Tony Burgess in *Sonoran Desert Plants* (1995). Very possibly, early hunters and gatherers preceded saguaros into the Sonoran Desert.

SAGUARO PARTS

The saguaro is one of nearly two thousand species of cacti. Cactus plants tend to grow in geometric shapes: hemispheres, spheres, disks, ovoids, ellipsoids, cylinders, and, of course, columns. This maximizes their volume and minimizes their surface area, reducing water loss in hot, dry climates. They are all perennials, and they all have areoles, special oval organs that stud cactus skin and produce clusters of spines, stems, blossoms, and fruit in the saguaro.

Zing! Spines stand out on these "vegetable porcupines," as the nature writer John Van Dyke dubbed them. Set in rows about one inch apart, each sharp, starry tuft contains one 2-inch central spine, stout as a darning needle, accompanied by two or three 1-inch secondary spines and a dozen shorter, thinner radial ones. Why spines? They may appear to serve only as defense against hungry, thirsty desert animals, but prickles also help to conserve moisture. Like miniature blinds, they shade the plant's skin and decrease evaporation. (Even a small amount of shadow is valuable in the desert.) Spines act as tiny windbreaks, too, and they insulate the plant in cold weather, particularly the frost-sensitive growing tips, where

Saguaro tip with protective, fuzzy "felt"
W. ROSS HUMPHREYS

the areoles are also swathed in a cream-colored fluff called felt. Felt probably supplies winter warmth as well as sun protection, and it may cushion the delicate growth areas from bites and blows.

At the top of a giant cactus, flexible new spines poke through this soft blond toupee. Unlike leaves, cactus spines do not replace themselves each spring. They are often as old as the spot on the cactus where they grow, and they show it, aging over the decades from rosy yellow to black to gray. The spines of young saguaros are relatively long and point downward to discourage small animals from eating the tender flesh. They also work as "drip-tips," concentrating raindrops around the young cactus. As the saguaro matures, the spines higher on its trunk tend to point outward rather than down, and the lower ones become sparse and brittle, until the base of the plant sheds its prickly armor and acquires a rough gray bark instead.

Spiny areoles of saguaro, 1857
GEORGE ENGELMANN

THE BIRDS AND THE BEES

All cactus plants can reproduce both sexually (from a seed) and vegetatively (from a cutting). In rare cases, a fallen saguaro arm may take root and grow in the ground, although it will always look like an arm and not like a young saguaro. Famously colorful as well as fragrant, cactus flowers consist of tepals—gradations between petals and sepals—arranged in a sunburst, pinwheel, or funnel shape. A saguaro blossom resembles a slender green ice cream cone with a fat white daisy plopped on top. It has a delicate aroma rather like sliced honeydew melon. All cactus fruits, which are often edible like those of the saguaro, develop below the tepals, not above, and enclose their seeds in a single chamber. If it germinates, each cactus seed generates two cotyledons, or seed leaves, and the life cycle begins again.

WATER AND WEATHER

If the saguaro were a conscious being, it would have three main obsessions: water, reproduction, and frost. From the tips of its roots to the top of its crown, it works to collect and conserve moisture, from which it creates flowers and fruit. In the Sonoran Desert, freezes threaten saguaros more than heat or drought. Periods of freezing weather shape individual cacti in spectacular ways, and they also determine the existence (or the end) of whole populations. Closely examined, nearly every strange and remarkable feature of the giant cactus somehow relates to these three overriding concerns. Most of the adaptations carry certain disadvantages, however.

To begin at the bottom, a saguaro root network radiates at least as far in all directions from the cactus as it is tall, and sometimes as much as one hundred feet away, but even the stubby taproots of mature saguaros only reach about three feet deep. Most roots are concentrated in the first few inches of soil, lying in wait for rain. "Water, water, water," they would whisper if they could. A severe drought may kill off the thinnest roots, but the system revives quickly, and new growth can begin within a day of a storm. Temporary rain-root networks gather the water, transport it to permanent root systems, and then wither away into the dust again.

On the negative side, shallow roots, insecurely anchored, can lead to a saguaro's downfall, especially when the ground is saturated and high winds blow. That's one reason why the giant cacti grow best in coarse, rocky, well-drained dirt, rather than sandy soil. Another drawback is that saguaros can get *too much* water, generally from over-enthusiastic gardeners in urban areas. Sumo saguaros often pop up alongside Southwestern streets, but excess fluid can actually bloat and kill them.

Delicate root systems also make it difficult to transplant saguaros. Young plants often are moved successfully, because their roots have not spread far, but once a saguaro is taller than 12 to 15 feet, the moving process usually damages too many roots for a saguaro to survive, though it may die slowly. Even given great care, only about 10 percent will live more than five years in the new location. Shallow roots are also vulnerable to damage if the soil around them becomes compacted by construction or traffic.

LIVE WATER TANKS

Water flows from the clouds to the soil to the roots to the plant tissues, where it slows down. Saguaros are live water-storage tanks with a simple structure. Their fleshy, absorbent pulp is supported by a ring of hard yet elastic ribs, joined at the base of the plant. (The anthropomorphic word "rib" commonly refers to the woody material inside the cactus, and to the vertical green ridges visible on the outside of a live plant.) Ribs, besides holding up perhaps six tons of cactus, also help the vascular system feed the plant. And while standing still, they move.

In the early days of the Desert Laboratory, a pioneering botanist named Effie Southworth Spaulding was the first scientist to catch saguaros in the act of performing what she called a "bellows-like action." During the winter of 1903 and 1904, she marked adjacent saguaro ribs with dots of India ink, and every day she measured the distances between dots with calipers. She also compared the changes in cactus girth with records of rainfall and artificial watering. Eureka!

"Expansion and contraction of the stem is correlated with water-supply," wrote Mrs. Spaulding in 1905.

Cross-sections sawed from saguaro trunks revealed several concentric rings of different kinds of tissue. A

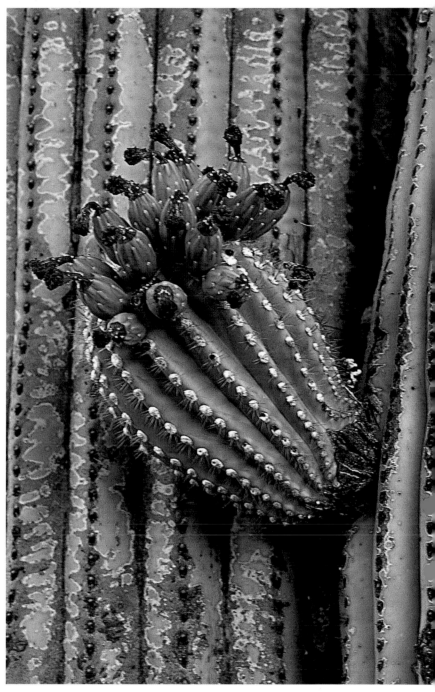

Accordion-pleated ribs expand and contract W. ROSS HUMPHREYS

strong, elastic outer layer protects an inner layer containing chlorophyll, and everything else except ribs consists of water storage cells. When a cactus uses or loses water, its storage cells shrink and its ribs draw closer together. Given a fresh supply, the cells plump up and the ribs spread. "It would be difficult to imagine a more perfect arrangement," Mrs. Spaulding concluded.

In fact saguaros can expand and contract by almost 50 percent. In the economy of the desert, saguaros are sometimes misers, sometimes spendthrifts. Miraculously they can hold enough water to bloom and set fruit after a year with absolutely no rain, or even after the main trunk is uprooted, making them literally the living dead. But reproduction is what they were saving for, after all.

Fledgling kestrels in saguaro boot nest TOM VEZO

THE INNOVATIVE SAGUARO

Effie Spaulding also saw interesting differences between the tops, bottoms and sides of saguaros. Her cross-sections showed her that at the top of a cactus the furrows between ribs were "nearly equal all around the stem." But as she moved her measurements down the trunk, she discovered a change: "The deeper and narrower furrows are on the south; and the wider, shallower ones are on the north side." And after a rain they behaved differently. "While the southern furrows may begin to expand earlier," she wrote, "the northern ones expand longer." This must be caused by a combination of temperature and light, she thought.

Other plant scientists have pointed out differences in the color and condition of the skin on the north and south sides. South-facing, or sunnier, sides are often browner and rougher, and more arms grow there. Saguaro buds cluster on the eastern quadrant of the stem and usually begin to bloom earliest there. Ripening fruit follows the same east-west pattern. When transplanting columnar cacti, it's crucial to orient them in the direction that they originally grew, for they have shaped themselves in many subtle ways to their harsh settings.

RUNNING THE SAGUARO ENGINE

While green leaves are pretty and shady, their thin, fluttering surfaces are quick to lose precious moisture. Dispensing with leaves altogether, as most cacti have done, enhances water conservation. Leaves serve a vital function as food factories for most plants, though. Through a lengthy evolution, the saguaro has transferred its chlorophyll (the green, food-making matter in leaves) to its trunk. Essentially its trunk is one big leaf.

Green cactus skin has a waxy covering called a cuticle. The cuticle helps slow water loss and is especially effective when the plant's pores, or stomates, are closed. Underneath the cuticle, saguaro chlorophyll makes food without dangerously depleting the plant's water reserves.

To perform photosynthesis, however, the cactus needs to draw carbon dioxide out of the same deathly dry desert air it tries to avoid. Here the saguaro works under cover of darkness. To minimize water loss, stomates close during the heat of the day and open when the temperature drops after the sun goes down.

But photosynthesis occurs only when there is light. Presto! With another trick of evolution, the saguaro converts carbon dioxide into an acid that can be stored for use under the next day's sun. This process, shared by some other succulent plants, is called crassulacean acid metabolism (often abbreviated to CAM), and it works best at low temperatures.

After a cool night, the saguaro is full of acid ready to be converted into food during the hot, bright daytime hours. The searing days and cloudless, cool evenings of the Sonoran Desert provide an ideal environment for saguaros and other plants relying on the CAM process. When stressed by drought, plants with CAM also have the ability to slow their engines to "idle," or go dormant by closing their stomates day *and* night. With their water locked up, they can live on stored resources until times improve. Then the cactus "engine" rapidly accelerates to full speed again.

But CAM has disadvantages, too. It causes both photosynthesis and growth to move slowly, which helps to explain why saguaros may take seventy-five years to produce their first crop of seeds and more than a century to reach their full height.

CRISTATE SAGUAROS

For reasons that are not completely understood, sometimes a cristate or "crested" saguaro develops. These specimens, roughly one in every two hundred thousand, have crown-like arms or tops. With their distinctive, fantastically shaped green headdresses, cristate saguaros look like alien invaders in the dry desert landscape. A genetic factor may be involved, according to Arizona-Sonora Desert Museum head horticulturist George Montgomery. "There are many other plants—not just cacti—that produce crested individuals," he pointed out.

Cristate saguaro, Desert Botanical Garden, Phoenix, Arizona KERRICK JAMES

ABOUT THOSE BOOTS

A woodpecker's beak, a rodent's tooth, a vandal's rock, or a storm that knocks off a saguaro arm . . . any attacker that breaks the waxy cactus skin is potentially deadly. To stanch water loss and stave off predators and infection, a saguaro, like other cacti, quickly corks its wounds with strong, dark, bark-like scar tissue. Calluses cover tiny nicks as well as raw stumps. Lining the nest holes carved out by Gila woodpeckers and gilded flickers, this tough stuff produces "boots" so resilient that they often outlast the rest of the plant. Woodpecker holes tend to occur in the lower, harder part of the saguaro trunk, because woodpeckers have stronger beaks than flickers, who usually choose higher, more tender areas. Flickers may tunnel through the top of a saguaro and damage its growth tip, perforating ribs and even occasionally killing the cactus. Woodpecker boots are smaller, flatter, and maybe more benign.

SUNBURN AND FREEZES

Sunburn is a saguaro skin condition. Technically called "epidermal browning" and still not fully understood, it may be related to sun exposure because it appears more commonly on the south sides of cacti. Concentrations of cuticle wax build up and inhibit photosynthesis, which must be a handicap to the plant. It remains to be seen whether browning relates to an atmospheric condition, such as ozone, or is merely a common symptom of aging. Probably cold is a bigger enemy than heat, however.

To a saguaro, freezing weather comes as either a master sculptor or the Grim Reaper. Many scientists believe that "catastrophic" freezes, which damage or kill large numbers of native plants, determine the plant's geographic range in southeastern Arizona and northern Sonora. Saguaros are closely constrained by the number of nights that the temperature drops below 32°F, and especially by the number of hours below 24°F, as botanist Janice Bowers determined.

"Catastrophic freezes usually occur within seventeen days of the winter solstice," she observed. "The longer nights mean that cold temperatures will be prolonged."

Wherever the temperature often drops below freezing for longer than half a day on average, there are no saguaros.

Temperatures below 21°F seriously harm giant cactus populations, killing very young ones and very old ones. Other signs of freeze damage include drooping arms, slender and leaning tops, scars, and curious deformations. A freeze can also decapitate a saguaro. Since catastrophic freezes often leave characteristic scars, sometimes scientists can date severe frosty spells by counting the number of swells and constrictions between such a scar and a stem tip. Like tree rings, these cactaceous ins and outs record annual growth. On a plant's physique they create what is sometimes called the "Mae West effect."

New growth rises from damaged stems TOM VEZO

Brittlebush and sunburned saguaro,
Organ Pipe Cactus National Monument, Arizona
CARR CLIFTON

GIANT CACTUS COUSINS

Cardón MEG QUINN

Many stout, strange, and spiky plants native to the Sonoran Desert are not cacti at all. These include yuccas, agaves, boojum trees (*Fouquieria columnaris*), ocotillos (*Fouquieria splendens*), and elephant trees (*Pachycormus discolor*).

While it's unique in the United States, the saguaro has several fascinating counterparts among the other giant cacti of Mexico and South America. One such "double" is the *cardón grande* of northern Argentina (*Trichocereus terschekii*), which has a saguaro-like profile and reaches heights of 40 feet. Its cousin *Trichocereus pascana* reminded botanists Britton and Rose of "a small *Carnegiea gigantea*" growing on the rocky hillsides of northern Argentina and Bolivia. Also reminiscent of the saguaro (or vice versa) are several members of the genus *Pachycereus* (literally "Thick Cereus") native to the southern Mexican states of Puebla and Oaxaca, including the gargantuan *Pachycereus chrysomallus*, and the slightly smaller *Pachycereus columna-trajani*, named for a Roman monument to the Emperor Trajan. *Cephalocereus macrocephalus* ("Big Head" cereus) is another tall columnar cactus from the Tehuacán area of Puebla in Mexico. Less monumental but more amusing in shape is the *Dendrocereus* ("Tree Cereus") of Cuba, which looks like a cross between a cactus and an apple tree, and the wacky *Jasminocereus* of the Galapagos Islands, apparently designed by Dr. Seuss.

In the Sonoran Desert, a number of members of the cereus branch of the cactus family are fairly close relatives of the saguaro, including hairbrush cactus, cardón, organ pipe cactus, barrel cactus, and senita.

Hairbrush cactus JIM HONCOOP

Hairbrush cactus
hecho cactus, cardón barbón
(Pachycereus pecten-aboriginum)

Growing only in the southernmost part of the Sonoran Desert, including the tip of Baja California, this medium-sized, many-armed columnar cactus has ten to twelve ribs and reaches up to 40 feet in height. Starting in January, its whitish flowers bloom in irregular vertical rows up and down the top few feet of each stem, and by summer they turn into fruits that are absolutely one of a kind. Dense with spines, they offer an incomparable dining experience: the chance to comb your hair with your dessert.

Cardón
sahuaso, sahueso, cardón pelón
(Pachycereus pringlei)

The cardón is a hulk. By its side even a saguaro looks wispy, almost ethereal—like a fashion model consorting with a heavy-weight prizefighter. In fact, the cardón is the truly gigantic giant cactus of the Sonoran Desert, often rising more than 60 feet high upon a trunk 5 feet in diameter. But though it is taller and weightier than the saguaro, the cardón is much more vulnerable to frost, and such tenderness limits its range to Baja California and the warm gulf coast of Sonora. It possesses fewer ribs than the saguaro (only ten to fifteen compared to the saguaro's twelve to thirty). Its fruit is spinier than a saguaro's, although the large white, night-blooming flowers of the two cacti are similar. Since the two plants have different silhouettes, they are distinguished easily at a distance. The more plentiful arms of the cardón start lower and rise at a sharper angle, hugging the thick central trunk, which they often outgrow.

Organ pipe cactus JIM HONCOOP

Organ pipe cactus
pitahaya, pitahaya dulce, órgano
(Stenocereus thurberi)

Many thin columns create the characteristic organ-pipe shape. Each "pipe" measures between 4 and 8 inches in diameter and has from twelve to nineteen ribs, more slender than those of the saguaro. Quite frost-sensitive, the growing tips of the organ pipe are easily killed, but the main plant often responds by sprouting new branches, so the total diameter of the cactus may reach 18 feet, or about as wide as it is high. In the southern parts of its range, where it grows in large stands on the warm plains of Mexico, it centers around a short trunk, but at its northern extreme in southwestern Arizona, most notably at Organ Pipe Cactus National Monument, the plant requires a sheltered habitat with a southern exposure, and the branches rise more or less straight out of the ground, like a mass of surprised snakes.

The only music the desert organ makes is the faint hiss of the wind through its dense spines. But on early summer nights it produces musky-scented, lavender-white flowers, followed in July by probably the most luscious (although bristly) fruit of any plant in its region.

Spiny barrel RUSS BISHOP

Barrel cactus
compass plant, *bisnaga* (also spelled *biznaga, visnaga, viznaga*)
(Ferocactus cylindraceus, Ferocactus emoryi, Ferocactus wizlizenii)

Juvenile barrel cacti may sometimes be mistaken for baby saguaros. They live in many of the same rocky, hot, and arid habitats as saguaros, and they are also columnar cacti, but they are not in fact particularly close relatives of *Carnegiea gigantea*. Armless except when injured, the biggest barrels can approach 10 feet in height, yet their stocky, heavily ribbed trunks rarely grow neatly perpendicular to the ground like saguaros. Instead, barrels tend to grow in a twist and to lean to the south, which gives them the nickname "compass plant." Why do they point south? Botanists have proposed several explanations, possibly all true to some degree. Warmer temperatures may increase flowering on the south side of the plant, causing it to lean toward the sun. But at the same time, the increased heat load and water stress on the south and southwest sides of the cactus may retard cell growth, which makes the barrel pucker and tilt.

Senita MEG QUINN

Senita
old man cactus, sinita, whisker cactus, *hombre viejo, cabeza de viejo, pitahayita*
(Lophocereus schottii)

This old man stands about as tall as an organ pipe cactus but is less massive, with five to ten ribs per 5-inch stem. As each stem ages, its upper spines grow 3 inches long and tangle together like tufts of gray hair. With less tolerance for cold than organ pipe cacti but more than cardóns, a very few senitas grow in Organ Pipe Cactus National Monument and elsewhere in southwestern Arizona; most of the old men live in Baja California and Sonora. Their pinkish or lavender flowers bloom at night in May and June, giving off an odor unpleasant to humans but attractive to moths and bats. A small edible fruit ripens in the fall.

Saguaro forest and Ragged Top, evening light,
Ironwood Forest National Monument, Arizona
STEPHEN INGRAM

THE GIANT CACTUS A TOHONO O'ODHAM CREATION TALE

Among the Desert People long ago there lived a girl who wanted to play toka all day long. (Toka is a women's game played with sticks, like hockey.) And this girl was such a good player that she always won.

Even after she had a baby, the young mother used to fill a big gourd with milk and set it beside her son. Then she stuck a bright feather in her hair and went from village to village playing toka just as she had always done, and she always won.

Now when this woman's child was left alone, he began to grow. He looked around and saw all the beads and feathers and baskets and pots that his mother had won playing toka. He saw the gourd full of milk. He drank the milk and grew larger and larger until finally he stood up, stuck a bright feather in his hair, and went to look for his mother.

At last, far away on the other side of the mountains, he came upon some women playing toka. Among them was a young woman who always won, and in her hair she wore a bright feather.

The boy asked a child who was playing nearby to go to the woman who wore a bright feather in her hair and say, "Your son has come, and he wants to see his mother."

The child carried the boy's message.

But the woman answered, "I will come as soon as I win this game."

The boy waited. Then he sent another child with the same message to his mother.

But she sent the same answer back.

Again the boy waited. And he was hungry. So he sent a third child to his mother begging her to come soon.

But this game of toka was very long. And the boy's mother answered the messenger, "Yes, yes, tell him I will come when I win this game."

When the third messenger returned, the boy became angry. "Help me find a tarantula's hole!" he said to the other children.

And they did.

"Help me sing!" he said.

So they formed a ring around him and began to dance and sing, and the boy sank into the tarantula's hole. With the first song he sank as far as his knees.

"Sing louder!" he cried. "Dance harder!"

And as they circled around him, singing and dancing, he kept on sinking into the earth. When only the boy's shoulders were above ground, one of the children ran to his mother, who was still playing toka, and told her, "Come quickly! The strange boy is almost buried in the tarantula's hole!"

The mother dropped her toka stick and ran as fast as she could. But she found nothing but a bright feather sticking out of a tarantula hole. And the sand was closing around the feather. The woman began to cry. And Coyote, who was passing, came to see what all the noise was about.

"My son has just been buried in the tarantula's hole!" she said. "Help me dig him out of the ground!"

So Coyote began to dig. He found that the boy was not very deep in the ground. Now, Coyote was hungry, and he didn't see why he should save this boy for a mother who had never done anything for her son. So he ate the boy. When the bones were clean, Coyote took them out of the hole and gave them to the woman along with the boy's bright feather.

"Someone must have eaten your son," he said. "This is all I could find."

The woman took the feather and looked at the bones. But unlike the feather, the bones of her son were not very bright, so she had no use for them. She told Coyote to bury them again, which he did.

Four days later, something green came out of the ground on the spot where the boy's bones were buried. In four more days, this green thing became a baby saguaro. It was the first saguaro, or giant cactus, in all the world. The first giant cactus was very strange. It was just a tall, thick, soft, smooth, green thing growing out of the ground.

All the Desert People and all the animals came to look at it. The children played around it and stuck sticks into it. This hurt Saguaro, and he put out long, sharp needles for protection so the children could not touch him. Then they took their bows and arrows and shot at him. This made Saguaro very angry, so he sank into the ground and went away where no one could find him and he could live in peace.

After Saguaro disappeared, the people were sorry and began looking for him. They hunted all over the mountains near the village. They asked all the animals and birds to help them. After a very long time, Crow told the people that he had seen a huge cactus where there was nothing but rocks and where no animals or people had ever hunted.

The chief called a council of all the animals and people, and he told the people to prepare four large round baskets. Then he told Crow to fly back to the giant cactus and what to do when he got there. When Crow reached the saguaro, he found the top of the giant cactus covered with red fruit full of juice and sugar. After gathering the fruit, Crow flew slowly back to the village.

The people were waiting.

And Crow put the cactus fruit into large pots, which were filled with water, placed on the fire, and kept boiling from sunrise to sunset. For four days this syrup was cooked. Then the chief told all the people to prepare for a special wine feast, which they had never had before.

The birds came dressed for the feast in red and black and yellow and blue. Rattlesnake came crawling up, painted in brilliant colors, too. But the birds gossiped and scolded and were jealous because Rattlesnake was as bright as they were, and they embarrassed him. So he rolled himself in ashes. And that is why, even nowadays, Rattlesnake's skin is marked with gray where the ashes caked onto his new paint. Meanwhile Gila Monster gathered pebbles and made himself a very beautiful, very hard coat. You can see it today, too, because he is still wearing it.

And then the people and animals and birds gathered around and drank the saguaro wine. And it was very strong. It made some sing. Others it put to sleep. Others were sick.

Nighthawk, who was dressed in gray and yellow, did not wish to spoil his fine feathers, so he brought a stick of cane to drink through. All the girls thought this was wonderful. And Grasshopper, who had borrowed Spider's web to make himself beautiful new wings, was filled with envy.

"I must do something to make people notice me!" he said.

So he pulled off one of his hind legs and stuck it on his head. And to this day, you will still sometimes see Grasshopper jumping around without a leg. When Nighthawk saw Grasshopper with his new headdress, he laughed so hard he split his mouth. And it stayed that way forever, which is why the nighthawk never flies in the daytime. His mouth is so big and white and ugly that he only

comes out after dark so nobody will see him. And that is why he darts past you so quickly in the evening.

As they kept on drinking, the birds began to fight. They pulled each other's feathers until the woodpeckers had bloody heads—just as you see them today.

When the chief saw the fighting and the bloody feathers, he decided that there should be no more wine feasts like that. So when all the wine was gone, he carefully gathered all the tiny black seeds of the giant cactus fruit, and he called a messenger to take the seeds away, off toward the rising sun.

This made the people unhappy, so they held a council and sent Coyote after the messenger. Coyote traveled very fast. He circled around the messenger and pretended to be coming from the opposite direction.

"Let me see what you have in your hand," said Coyote.

"No, that is impossible," said the messenger.

But Coyote begged, "Just one little look!"

At last, after much coaxing, he persuaded the messenger to open one finger of the hand that held the saguaro seeds. Then Coyote complained that he could not see enough.

"Open just one more finger!" he said.

And so, little by little, the messenger's hand was opened.

Suddenly, Coyote struck the messenger's hand and the little seeds of the giant cactus flew into the air. The wind caught up the seeds and scattered them all over the south side of the mountains.

And this is why giant saguaros still grow in the land of the Desert People, and always on the southern slopes of the mountains. And ever since that time, once a year, when the fruit is ripe, the people and the animals still feast.

Note: The story of the first saguaro occurs in many versions, oral and written, including Lumholtz (New Trails in Mexico, 1912). This one is adapted from a version recorded in the early twentieth century and first published with many other O'odham tales in Long Ago Told by Harold Bell Wright (1929). A popular novelist, Wright probably imagined himself following in the footsteps of the Brothers Grimm when he wrote this tale, which reveals almost as much about Wright as about his Native American subjects.

Saguaro cactus at sunrise, Organ Pipe Cactus National Monument, Arizona
Carr Clifton

3

From Seeds to Skeletons

Saguaros are true survivors. "A giant cactus that has reached adulthood has escaped many, many adversities," observed the Latin American cactus experts Helia Bravo Hollis and Leia Scheinvar. John Van Dyke was another admirer: "They have no idea of dying without a struggle," he wrote. "They are marvellous engines of resistance."

If we could follow one particular saguaro throughout its lifetime, we'd begin with a black speck. Each purplish-red saguaro fruit is only about the size of a fig and weighs from one to three ounces, but its crimson pulp contains around two thousand crunchy little pinheads, each one bigger than a poppy seed but smaller than a sesame seed. A full-grown saguaro may bear up to one hundred fruits and generate as many as two hundred thousand possible offspring in a single year. Yet every seed faces enormous risks, and very few live to grow up.

Unlike dog years, saguaro years move very slowly. A full saguaro life span of 175 to two hundred years is much longer than a single human life. But saguaros at various stages coexist in a place like Saguaro National Park, so we can reconstruct the biography of a single cactus.

Curling ribs on skeletal saguaro,
Saguaro National Park East, Arizona
RANDY PRENTICE

Gila woodpecker and saguaro cactus flower TOM VEZO

The appearance of the saguaro fruit tips off a frenzy of excitement among the animal residents of the desert. As each fruit ripens, it splits to reveal its contents, a moist and luscious miracle in the drought before the summer rains. From late May to mid-July, the race is on. The sun bakes our tiny seed, the wind shakes it, and soon the predators arrive. Saguaro fruit may ripen 50 feet above the ground, so wings provide a great advantage to hungry bats and many kinds of birds, especially doves, woodpeckers, and finches. When the fruit finally hits the ground, it is seized and devoured by everything from harvester ants to rodents, rabbits, and ground squirrels, and on up the food chain to the larger omnivorous mammals such as javelinas (distant relatives of swine, properly known as collared peccaries), coyotes, and human beings.

Suddenly that one particular seed disappears down the gullet of a white-winged dove. But is it really gone forever?

Not quite. Our seed is lucky, so first it's swallowed and then it's spilled to the ground by the dove as she coughs up saguaro fruit to feed her two gray chicks. Hard-coated saguaro seeds may also pass unharmed through the digestive tracts of various animals, which help saguaros by dropping prefertilized seeds in areas that wind and water, two other powerful distributors, might not reach. Weather is one of the most important factors in successful saguaro reproduction. Most years, the majority of seeds are cast around July 1, just as the rainy season provides the jolt of warmth and moisture that saguaros need to germinate.

Despite all the distribution, however, most of the seeds disappear within a few weeks. Some are carried off by insects or consumed by animals. Some fall below the mother

plant into rocky crevices. Some blow out of reach of animals or are washed away in a storm. Saguaro ecologists Steenbergh and Lowe estimated that fewer than ten out of every thousand seeds end up in a good enough site to have a chance to become a plant. Perhaps four of those ten will germinate, and only one will sprout into a seedling.

But our fortunate seed lands in precisely the right conditions, a sheltered spot on a bajada, or rocky slope, leading down from a desert mountain. Not only does the seed need appropriate soil—gravelly and sandy rather than clayey—and warm temperatures, but it also needs light, so it can't be buried more than a few millimeters deep. Without moisture it won't germinate, but that moisture must come at exactly the right time, preferably late July or early August. Saguaro seeds do best with one or two rainstorms within a few days of germination. Since ours is lucky, a thunderstorm comes along, and about five days later, the black speck sends up two tiny, plump, pointed "ears," which are the first and last tender green leaves the saguaro will ever grow.

FORTUNE-COOKIE STAGE

"The seedling plant," wrote Engelmann, who first described it in 1848, "is globose, grows very slowly, and is rather delicate." The brand-new saguaro looks like a minuscule yellow-green fortune cookie, "barely larger than a grain of sand," as Steenbergh and Lowe said. The fortune-cookie stage is the first of the seven ages of the saguaro, and the most vulnerable. The highest mortality rate in the saguaro's lifetime comes during its first five or six weeks. Frost and heat can be equally fatal. Even a heedless lizard might crush a seedling, not to mention a cow hoof. But to be noticed by an animal could be even worse. "The tiny capsules of acid water stored in the plump, spineless hypocotyl constitute a most attractive morsel for the thirsty and hungry animals," remarked D. T. MacDougal, the first director of the Desert Laboratory, writing in 1908. He calculated that "not one seedling in a million survives the first year in consequence."

Fortune cookie

NURSE PLANTS

The dove did our seed a favor by spilling it underneath a palo verde tree. Young saguaros generally need to grow beneath the cover of a tree or a shrub. These protectors, or "nurse plants," moderate the conditions of early life for the baby saguaros and for other types of cactus, too. Anyone exploring the desert will find many small cacti hidden away like untouchable Easter eggs under shrubs and trees. Nurse plants decrease extreme heat, retain moisture in the soil, buffer against frost, and prevent most trampling by animals. (A certain mesquite tree in the Altar Valley of northern Sonora shelters an enormous "elementary school" of eighty-three young saguaros.) Even a rock can

Young "wine bottle" saguaro bearing fruit,
Saguaro National Park West, Arizona
RANDY PRENTICE

Young saguaros under foothills palo verde nurse plant RANDY PRENTICE

nurse along an infant cactus. "Rocks concentrate and prolong availability of soil moisture," Steenbergh and Lowe pointed out. A nurse rock also absorbs daytime heat and re-radiates it at night, working like a furnace for any small cactus nearby.

The new seedling starts as a succulent little "cookie" but within a week it develops a stem and sprouts its first areoles, complete with tiny spines. Still, it remains technically a seedling throughout its first year, and this period is the second-riskiest time of its life. Unlike their parents, baby saguaros have very little storage capacity, so a dry spell will shrivel them. And to a black longhorn beetle, a juicy green saguaro sprout *is* a cookie. To a pair of Gambel's quail, herding their chicks underneath a palo verde tree, a saguaro seedling is a refreshing canteen. But the lucky seedling happens to be hidden by a pebble, and no lethal frost reaches under its nurse plant, so the seedling reaches its first birthday and graduates to the second stage of a saguaro's life.

HEIGHT DOES NOT EQUAL AGE

Now hairy with fine spines, a yearling saguaro looks like a microscopic leaf-green cactus, not a cookie . . . but not yet a saguaro, either. Any saguaro at this second stage is round and knobby (in botanical terms, "hemispherical" and "tuberculate"), and 40 to 60 percent of its mass lies underground. Its height may vary tremendously, depending on the location and weather where it grows, from a tenth of an inch in a difficult place to a full inch in a greenhouse. This remains true throughout the life cycle of all saguaros, making it impossible to gauge their ages with much accuracy by their height. Saguaros of a similar size may in fact be quite different ages.

"It is difficult to find the very young Sahuaros," wrote Forrest Shreve, the dean of Sonoran Desert botanists during the first half of the twentieth century. Saguaro census takers work on their hands and knees, using magnifying glasses to detect what Steenbergh and Lowe describe as "a small, concealing tuft of tan-colored spines." Technically a "tuberculate juvenile," our tuft under the palo verde tree still has a long way to go.

Tuft

A tuft makes an easy mouthful for a white-throated wood rat, or pack rat, one of the rare mammals that can subsist entirely on a diet of cactus tissue. (Most animals tolerate an occasional emergency cactus meal, but consuming too much of the oxalic acid in cactus tissue causes kidney failure.) With its high surface-to-volume ratio, a tuft is still very vulnerable to frost and drought but ours, being one in a million, survives.

PINCUSHION STAGE

By age seven, it has developed ten to fourteen little ribs and the fluted appearance of a more mature saguaro. It's approximately an inch high, and more than half of its stem now shows above the ground, but its shape is still basically round. It is no longer a tuft. It has reached its third age, and it becomes a "spherical juvenile," or pincushion.

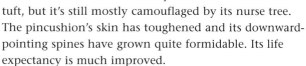

Pincushion

As a pincushion, the cactus grows faster. For the next five to ten years, it steadily expands, first in all directions and then gradually upward into an ellipsoid shape. It can't hide as easily as it did when it was a mere tuft, but it's still mostly camouflaged by its nurse tree. The pincushion's skin has toughened and its downward-pointing spines have grown quite formidable. Its life expectancy is much improved.

When a pincushion reaches a height of 6 or 7 inches, it begins to add new ribs, which stand out clearly as forks in the vertical rows of bristles on the surface of any mature saguaro. Each marks a little chapter in its history. So does a nick, now healed, where a curve-billed thrasher once tasted our young cactus and moved on.

BLIMPS AND TORPEDOES

The fourth age of saguaros begins when the lucky seed becomes a teenager. By its fourteenth summer, 85 percent of its stem rises above the ground, and it is 2 feet high. Like a human teenager, it develops a new figure, elongating from a ball into a blimp shape that narrows where it meets the ground. The tops of young blimp saguaros are thickly thatched with crisscrossed spines springing from patches of hairy felt. Besides warding off attackers, the spines provide a natural "straw hat" against the sun. Both spines and felt probably insulate sensitive growth zones, so any saguaro over three feet high is fairly frost-resistant.

Blimp

Torpedo

During the next few decades, the fast-growing blimp stretches into a torpedo shape and reaches the fifth age of saguaros.

But it is still a juvenile until the spring of its thirty-seventh year. By this time it's more than six feet tall, but it weighs twice as much as a big man. Its increasing mass is supported by fifteen to twenty ribs and protected by 3- to 4-inch central spines, which point straight out from its sides.

The torpedo saguaro has broken through the canopy of the palo verde tree, which lost a branch in the process. As the branch fell, it scratched the cactus, but the wound is well covered with gray callus. Several "waists" in the saguaro's circumference are mementos of freezes or droughts that briefly slowed its growth. The tip of the torpedo saguaro is heavily insulated with felt, because the areoles there are active.

FIRST BLOSSOMS AND SEEDS

Finally, in the middle of April, one areole begins to swell, and soon it thrusts up the youthful plant's first bud, followed by its first white wax trumpet of a flower, and then its first fruit. The lucky seed has created seeds of its own. This is a major landmark in the saguaro's biological existence. It's officially an adult saguaro, although it remains a torpedo shape.

From now on the young adult saguaro spends April, May, June, and July wearing a lumpy headdress. Many lumps are green (buds and unripe fruit), some are white (flowers), and by high summer they're a mixture of red and black (ripe fruit, mistaken for "red flowers" in 1852 by the explorer-botanist C.C. Parry, and often fooling people ever since). Insects, birds, and animals flock around the cactus, some playing double roles as pollinators and seed scatterers.

At first glance a saguaro blossom seems designed to attract nocturnal visitors, for it produces fragrance, nectar, and pollen throughout the single night it blooms. The flower is self-sterile, so it must attract animals bringing outside pollen in order to set fruit. Large, white, and high, it looks like a beacon for nectar-sipping bats, and it is. The lesser long-nosed bat (*Leptonycteris curasoae*) drinks the sweet nectar and eats the nutritious pollen of several tropical columnar cacti, including the saguaro. But some saguaros live north of the bats' range, and each saguaro blossom is also open during part of a day.

Researchers have discovered that the big white funnels are not only "bat flowers," as Mark Dimmitt, director of natural history at the Arizona-Sonora Desert Museum, put it, but "bee flowers" and "bird flowers" as well. Possibly other insects, such as beetles, also participate. During the day, nonnative honeybees as well as several indigenous desert bees gather nectar and pollen. White-winged doves begin their vigils over the tops of saguaros before any buds open and continue to watch and nibble—and squabble—till the last fruit falls. And probably the full story of giant-cactus pollination is not known even yet.

Bees pollinating saguaros W. ROSS HUMPHREYS

Curve-billed thrasher TOM VEZO

WINE BOTTLES AND ARM BUDS

Our thriving young-adult saguaro, sixty years old and 12 feet tall, looks more prosperous than its shorter nurse tree, which is struggling to compete for water now. Reproduction demands so much energy that the young saguaro's growth rate slows, and its figure changes again as it moves into the sixth age of saguaros. The top of the cactus thins, resulting in a wine-bottle shape. And one day an areole puts out an arm bud about seven feet above the ground on the south side of the wine-bottle saguaro.

Within as little as three years, the arm bud bears fruit of its own, as do other arms that soon develop about the same distance from the ground. A giant cactus in a meager setting may never grow arms, but by multiplying their potential number of seeds, those that do branch greatly increase their chance of successful reproduction. And now the Gila woodpeckers and the gilded flickers move in.

Wine bottle

ANCIENT GIANT

As the saguaro's arms grow longer, more bird holes appear. Armed now with six branches and producing one hundred fruits a year, the lucky saguaro marks its first century, and it passes from the wine-bottle into the seventh age of saguaros: the crazy candelabrum. Candelabra saguaros are fully mature, and they remain candelabra till the end of their lives. They continue to grow slowly for perhaps another hundred years, so their shapes are not static but continually remodeled. The years have added more ripples to this one's trunk and frost has made two of its arms droop in odd loops. Gray bark encircles its base, and the sun browns its south side. Its nurse tree dies of drought but the saguaro, tanked up with water, lives on.

The candelabrum now becomes vulnerable to new dangers, mostly from sudden catastrophes. A freak windstorm sweeps through the rain-saturated desert, toppling a nearby cactus, but the lucky saguaro escapes with only the loss of an arm. Fluid drips from the wound, first watery and then dark from the same substance, melanin, that colors human skin. Soon the stump seals itself with cork. Now the cactus has twenty-two boots instead of twenty-three, and it generates fewer fruits. But within two years of the disaster it starts a new crop of shorter arms higher on its trunk.

Through rainstorm after rainstorm, its luck holds. Lightning electrocutes other saguaros in a single stroke but somehow spares this one, even when it passes the 50-foot mark and becomes an ancient giant pocked with forty bird holes. One frosty January its top begins to lean, but the cactus actually manages to grow a round new branch from the damaged spot, as though it's balancing a ball on its head.

ENDINGS AND BEGINNINGS

Candelabrum

As the saguaro reaches the end of its life cycle, parts of it sag—first one arm, then another. Then a freeze decapitates it, and bacterial necrosis, a plant infection, sets in. The ancient saguaro continues to bloom, sparsely now, but never failing up to the very last spring of its two hundred years. When it finally crashes to the ground one windy night, it shatters the bleached remains of the palo verde that once protected it.

This is not really the end, however. A dead saguaro is a bonanza for the microbe, fungus, and insect population all around. "What better pond is there in the desert?" asked entomologist Carl A. Olson. In a single cubic foot of rotting saguaro once analyzed at the University of Arizona, 413 arthropods formed a complete ecosystem. Stripped eventually of watery flesh, the saguaro skeleton, with boots tucked inside it, lies bare under the sun, occasionally shading a rabbit or an annual plant, or furnishing useful supplies to a human passerby.

And in another way it is not the end. Near the skeleton of the lucky saguaro, sheltered beneath bushes and trees, or standing alone, are fortune cookies, tufts, pincushions, blimps, torpedoes, wine bottles and crazy candelabra, all moving slowly into the future together.

Saguaro skeleton,
Superstition Mountains, Arizona
KERRICK JAMES

A Saguaro Year

June / Junio

Hahshani Mashad (Tohono O'odham)
"Saguaro Month," "Saguaro Harvest Month"
Harsany Paihitak Marsat (Pima)
"Saguaro Harvest Moon"

About June 21: Summer Solstice
June 24: *El día de San Juan* (Feast day of St. John the Baptist, associated in Hispanic tradition with the first day of the summer rains)

Hot, with low humidity. First possibility of summer thunderstorms. Normal high: 99.6°F. Normal low: 67.9°F. Normal precipitation: 0.20 inch. (Normal annual total: 12.0 inches.)

Saguaros blossom, pollination takes place, fruit ripens, and seedfall begins. Time to move to cactus camps to gather, eat, and process fruit.

George H. H. Huey

July / Julio

Jukiabig Mashad (Tohono O'odham)
"Giant Cactus Ripe Month"
Tcokiapik Marsat (Pima)
"Rainy Moon"

Hot and wet. Summer rains bring higher humidity and occasional flooding. Normal high: 99.4°F. Normal low: 73.6°F. Normal precipitation: 2.37 inches.

Saguaro blossoming ends, most fruit is ripe, seed dispersal accelerates, and germination begins. From the middle of July to the first week of August is the best time for a saguaro seed to germinate. Established saguaros gather water and grow. Animals and insects eat saguaro fruit and seedlings. Tall saguaros face danger from lightning, saturated soil, and high winds. With saguaro harvest complete, traditional desert people "sing down the rain" throughout the summer with the *nawai't* or saguaro wine feast.

August / Agosto

Shopol Eshabig Mashad (Tohono O'odham)
"Short Planting Month"
Rsopol Usapik Marsat (Pima)
"Big Rain Month"

Summer rainy season continues. Normal high: 96.8°F. Normal low: 72.1°F. Normal precipitation: 2.19 inches.

The last saguaro fruit ripens, seeds germinate, seedlings and mature stems grow. Lightning and wind danger is still high.

Randy Prentice

September / Septiembre

Washai Gak Mashad (Tohono O'odham)
Varsa Kakatak Marsat (Pima)
"Dry Grass Month"

Slightly cooler and drier. Thunderstorms become less frequent. Normal high: 95.3°F. Normal low: 67.5°F. Normal precipitation: 1.67 inches.

Saguaro growth and seed germination continue, but most seedlings perish. Lightning and wind danger lessens.

October / Octubre

Wi'ihanig Mashad (Tohono O'odham)
"Month of Persisting Vegetation," "Month of Winds,"
"Month When Cold Touches Mildly," "Surviving Month"
Vi-ihainyik Marsat (Pima)
"Windy Moon"

Hot days alternate with cooler, drier ones, with a few late storms. Normal high: 84.3°F. Normal low: 56.6°F. Normal precipitation: 1.06 inches.

Saguaros stop growing and go dormant. Remaining seedlings at high risk.

November / Noviembre

Kehg S-hohpijig Mashad (Tohono O'odham)
"Month When It Is Really Getting Nice and Cold," "Month of Fair Cold," "Month of Pleasant Cold," "Month of Low Cold"
Huhokiapk' Marsat (Pima)
"Moon When Winter Begins"

Temperate days, cool nights. Slight chance of rain or frost. Normal high: 72.7°F. Normal low: 45.6°F. Normal precipitation: 0.67.

Saguaros are dormant. Cold weather may produce freeze damage or kill small saguaros.

Sunset, San Pedro Valley, Arizona Jack Dykinga

DECEMBER / DECIEMBRE

E Da Wa'ugad Mashad (Tohono O'odham)
"Month of the Inner Bone" [i.e., the backbone of winter],
  "Month of Great Cold"
Ku-utco s'hupitcik, Ka-amak (Pima)
"Moon When the [Mesquite] Leaves Fall," "Big Winter"

Weather ranges from warm to very cold. Snow is possible, even at low elevations. Normal high: 64.3°F. Normal low: 39.8°F. Normal precipitation: 1.07 inches.
    Saguaros are dormant. During winter rain they store water, but less than they do in summer. For seventeen days before and seventeen days after Dec. 21, catastrophic freezes, lethal to saguaros, are most frequent in the Sonoran Desert.

THOMAS WIEWANDT

JANUARY / ENERO

Gi'i hodag Mashad (Tohono O'odham)
"Month When Animals Have Lost
  Their Fat," "Month When Animals
  Go into Heat"
Aufpa Hiasik, Kamaki (Pima)
"Cottonwood Flowers Moon," "Gray Moon"

Winter rains, snowfall and catastrophic freezes possible. Normal high: 63.0°F. Normal low: 38.6°F. Normal precipitation: 0.87 inches.
    Saguaros remain largely dormant, except during rain, when minor growth may occur.

FEBRUARY / FEBRERO

Kohmagi Mashad (Tohono O'odham)
"Gray Month"
Aufpa I-ivakitak, Tcu-utaki (Pima)
"Cottonwood Leaves Moon," "Green Moon"

Warm as well as cool days, with rain and a few freezes possible. Spring is coming. Normal high: 67.8°F. Normal low: 41.0°F. Normal precipitation: 0.70 inches.
    Saguaros continue to resist frost damage and stay mostly dormant. Wildflower season may begin, depending on rainfall. Birds start pecking nest holes in tall saguaros.

MARCH / MARZO

Chehdagi Mashad (Tohono O'odham)
"Green Month"
Koi I-ivakitak Marsat, Oam Marsat (Pima)
"Mesquite Leaves Moon," "Yellow Moon"

Spring comes to the desert, although snowfall is still possible. Normal high: 72.8°F. Normal low: 44.6°F. Normal precipitation: 0.72 inches.
    Annuals and smaller cacti bloom first. In a wet year, the giant cacti are well stocked with water for their upcoming bloom. Elf owls and other birds build nests in saguaro cavities.

APRIL / ABRIL

Oam Mashad (Tohono O'odham)
"Yellow Month," "Yellow-Orange Month"
Koi Hiasik Marsat, Oam Marsat (Pima)
"Mesquite Flowers Moon," "Yellow Moon"

Peak of springtime, warm and generally dry. Normal high: 81.2°F. Normal low: 50.4°F. Normal precipitation: 0.30 inches.
    Starting in lower, warmer locations, saguaros bud. Within a few weeks, blooming begins and continues into June. Bees swarm, some moving into saguaro boots. Hawks may nest on saguaro branches. During April, May, and June, last year's surviving saguaro seedlings may shrivel to half of their winter size.

MAY / MAYO

Kai Chukalig Mashad (Tohono O'odham)
"Month When Saguaro Seeds Are Turning
  Black," "Painful Month"
*Pe kany Paihitak Marsat, Ka-ak Marsat,
  Kai Tcokolik Marsat* (Pima)
"Wheat Harvest Moon," "Strong Moon,"
  "Black Seeds on Saguaros Moon"

GEORGE H. H. HUEY

Hot, cloudless, and dry. The temperature usually exceeds one hundred degrees this month. Normal high: 89.9°F. Normal low: 58.0°F. Normal precipitation: 0.18 inches.
    Saguaros are in full bloom, and pollinators ranging from bees to lesser long-nosed bats are active day and night. Birds also participate. Early blossoms now form fruit, and black saguaro seeds, displayed in split fruit, indicate ripeness. In ancient desert societies, this month was "painful" because food and water ran short. Every desert person and many of their neighbors, such as the Apaches, kept an eye on the saguaro, organ pipe, and cardón or pitahaya fruit. Cactus New Year was coming!

Tohono O'odham calendar information from Lumholtz (1912), Underhill (1939, 1979), Saxton and Saxton (1969); Pima calendar information from Russell (1908); weather data measured (1961-1990) at Tucson International Airport by the National Weather Service.

HOW TO END A SEASON

Ofelia Zepeda

Food is put in place for the ancestors.

Prayer sticks are buried for the saguaro, for the seasons,
   for the earth.

Songs are sung for the spiritual health of everyone, everything.

And in the fading light of a bright summer day

the people sit down to eat and visit.

There are decorations paying commercial homage to the saguaro.

Balloons with smiling little saguaros on them,

and others in large type reading, "Saguaro," and in smaller
   print, "credit union."

Amid the festive decorations the sun lowers on the horizon,

colors begin to show.

The people are treated to stews of chile,

different types of beans, tortillas and breads.

Salad and chicken for the kids.

And of course there is ever-present ciolim for everyone.

Marigold, lavender, and a touch of hibiscus hang above the
   dry, desert mountains.

The singers' soft voices carry the songs across the desert floor.

To the east, a bright star takes a long trailing fall, the glow
   is wide and slow.

The people point.

The gohimeli songs begin.

They step to the rhythm, feel the beat of the earth.

They look at all that is around them, and drink the wine
   for the goodness of the earth.

As the celebration continues,

a toy-like machine stumbles across the landscape of
   a red planet.

NASA knocks on the window of America's childhood memories

with Rover, Yogi and Barnacle Bill.

ciolim: cooked cholla buds

gohimeli: traditional dance and songs

From *Red Ink*, Vol. 7, No. 2, Spring 1999. © 1997 by Ofelia Zepeda.
Reprinted by permission of the author.

Ofelia Zepeda is Professor of Linguistics at the University of Arizona,
a MacArthur Fellow, and a distinguished poet. She is considered the
foremost authority on Tohono O'odham language and literature.

Ofelia Zepeda TONY CELENTANO

4

Saguaros and Ancient Cultures

To the people of many different cultures over the last ten thousand years, the saguaro was more than a curious plant. It was a grocery store, a lumberyard, and a money tree. And it was sacred.

Sonoran Desert groups known to have used saguaro products within historic times include the Tohono O'odham, Pimas, Southeastern Yavapais, Northwestern Yavapais, Western Yavapais, Hualapais, Western Apaches, Chiricahua Apaches, Seris, Maricopas, Halchidhomas, Opatas, and Yaquis, as well as the Hispanic residents of the area. Probably the Quechans (Yumas), Mayos, Mohaves, and Warihios did, too.

Prized during its lifetime for its fruit, the cactus yielded at least twelve different food products that could be eaten or traded. After its death, it was valued for its boots (little Seri girls used to keep their dolls in them) and its ribs. The smooth, symmetrical, durable wood of the giant cactus supplied handy materials for fences, cradles, canes,

Maricopa Indian women among saguaros, 1907
EDWARD S. CURTIS

Circumpolar star trails and Leonid meteor shower, Saguaro National Park East, Arizona JAMES S. WOOD / ARIZONA DAILY STAR

or calendar sticks (record-keeping poles marked with symbols for important events). Ground saguaro seeds could help to tan a hide, and a concoction of saguaro flowers could waterproof a pot. A hot poultice of saguaro flesh relieved the pain of rheumatism.

The giant cactus had symbolic value, too. Its image appears in basketry and jewelry and even among the stars, for the Seri word for "harvesting pole" is also the name of

the constellation Ursa Major, or the Big Dipper, which the Seris saw as a group of people picking cactus fruit. The Tohono O'odham called the Big Dipper the Cactus Puller, and the Hualapais and Havasupais have similar names for the constellation.

Varying by region and storyteller, several legends explain the creation of the saguaro. Some say that the first giant cactus sprang from the drops of perspiration that fell into the dust from the brow of I'itoi, the O'odham Creator and "Elder Brother." Some suggest that I'itoi placed the beads of sweat on the ground intentionally, as symbols of the hard, hot work of the harvest. The complex, deeply serious creation story of the Pimas and Tohono O'odham contains yet another account of the first saguaro, while a Seri folktale is more humorous. Saguaros were also set to music in an ancient Tohono O'odham song:

> The big mothers stand there.
> The big mothers stand there.
> Whitely they flower.
> Black [the blossoms] dry.
> Red they ripen.
>
> (Recorded by Ruth Underhill in *Papago Indian Religion*, 1946)

Above all, wine made from saguaro fruit inspired an important religious and cultural experience for the Pimas and Tohono O'odham and probably for their neighbors and predecessors in the Sonoran Desert as well.

SAGUAROS AND PEOPLE IN PREHISTORY

"There is both direct and indirect evidence of prehistoric saguaro use," said Sue Wells of the Western Archeological Conservation Center of the National Park Service in Tucson. Traces of fruit, ribs, and boots all turn up in the archaeological record.

"In just about every prehistoric site excavated in the Tucson Basin, saguaro seeds are among the three or four commonest seeds that we find," said Jonathan Mabry,

a research archeologist with Desert Archaeology, Inc. of Tucson. "This is true all the way from the four-thousand-year-old Desert Archaic hunter-gatherer sites through the early farmers, the Hohokam, and the protohistoric cultures." The other common seeds, he noted, are mesquite, corn, and grass.

In central Arizona, too, people depended on saguaro fruit. Almost 30 percent of all seeds recovered during excavations of the Hohokam village at Snaketown, near Phoenix, were from *Carnegiea gigantea*. Archeologist Emil Haury, who directed the dig at Snaketown, speculated that vinegar made from saguaro fruit might have provided the acid used by Hohokam craftsmen to etch decorative designs on seashells. (In his experiments, saguaro vinegar worked perfectly.)

Impressions of saguaro ribs burned into adobe show that cactus wood was used in prehistoric buildings. Placed over his face, a saguaro boot accompanied a Hohokam man into the afterlife when he was buried in Ventana Cave in southwestern Arizona. Another remarkable boot was discovered in a packrat midden in Colossal Cave, near Tucson. This prehistoric fanny pack still contains a hunter's tangled wad of rawhide deer sinew, probably once used to lash stone points onto arrows. Since Colossal Cave was an ancient shrine, perhaps the saguaro boot's owner left it there as an offering.

Ancient saguaro boot hunter's pack
JONATHAN MABRY

Saguaro rib fence and harvesting stick W. ROSS HUMPHREYS

WINE IN THE DESERT

Other evidence of saguaro use comes from Native American oral traditions and from European travelers, who noticed that native peoples consumed cactus, including saguaro fruit—most notably, or notoriously, as wine. Referring to the people of northern Sonora in 1540, Coronado's chronicler, Pedro de Castañeda de Nájera, wrote: "They drink the juice of the pitahaya, a fruit of big thistles which opens like the pomegranate. They become stupefied with this drink." In the late 1600s the Jesuit missionary Father Eusebio Francisco Kino observed that Sonorans would drop everything, even neglecting livestock, when the cactus fruit was ripe.

"These Indians live free from drunkenness, more so than others," wrote another Jesuit missionary, Juan Velarde, in 1716. "Only during the season of the *pitahaya*, in such localities where it may be found, do they happen to make wine out of it. This might last them two or three days. They do not use it to the excess that other nations do."

Many travelers praised the flavorful, valuable syrup made from cactus fruit, comparing it to honey and molasses. But they did not appreciate the religious significance of the desert wine, even though sacramental wine occurs in the Judeo-Christian tradition, and sacred drinks are common worldwide. As in the Greek Bacchanalia, religion and wild behavior merged in the desert wine feasts that were believed to bring essential, life-giving rains.

Another Jesuit, Joseph Ochs, visited the region in the mid-seventeenth century and found "an agreeable beverage" made from the "blood-red" juice of the pitahaya fruit, which Ochs thought "would be found palatable even by the finest gentleman." Father Salvatierra, a colonial Spanish missionary in California, remarked that "the three pitahaya months resemble[d] the carnival in some parts of Europe [with] feastings, dancings, entertainments, buffooneries, and comedies."

FEASTING ON FRUIT

Accustomed to a feast-or-famine existence, the desert people ate as much fruit as they could when it was ripe. "With some this food agrees so well that they become corpulent during that period," wrote Jacob Braegert in the eighteenth century, "and for this reason I was some-times unable to recognize at first sight individuals other-wise perfectly familiar to me, who visited me after having fed three or four weeks on these pitahayas."

The saguaro fruit is quite large; much bigger, for example, than a wild grape or strawberry. Its pulp and seeds supply about thirty-four calories, as well as moisture, fiber, flavor and crunch. A tablespoon of seeds contains approximately thirty-seven calories and significant amounts of fat,

protein, and vitamin C. In ancient days, the fruit was the only sweet food available (sugar, concentrated in the stringy material around the seeds, accounts for 6.6 percent of the dry weight of the fruits). It also came as the first fresh food for many months. Time was counted by harvests; three years were "three pitahayas."

Living among the Seris along the Gulf of California in the late nineteenth century, ethnologist William J. McGee calculated that cactus fruit, including saguaro, cardón, and prickly pear, made up about 9 percent of the Seri diet and was probably their most important wild food. It was also a mainstay for the Tohono O'odham, whose community saguaro harvest has been estimated at six hundred thousand pounds of fruit annually. Probably the fruit was also a staple for the Pimas, who lived close to cactus forests, although they did more farming than their desert relatives. For groups less dependent on desert wild food and summer rainfall, cactus products probably amounted to occasional treats or trade items.

MAKING THE HARVEST

In bygone days a Tohono O'odham family had a winter home near water, a summer home or farm, and a cactus camp. Without summer rains, agriculture was impossible. On the way to their fields, people might stop in the cactus groves for a few weeks while women and children picked and prepared the fruit and men hauled water and tended the livestock. Among the Seris, however, men and boys helped to gather fruit.

Both the Seris and Tohono O'odham began the harvest with a ritual. With the Seris the season started when the first cactus buds were joyously carried into camp (but first-born children must not touch them, or their human lives would be shortened). When the first fruit ripened, the Seris dabbed the red pulp on both cheeks and the tip of the nose for good luck. Among the Tohono O'odham, each person took the first ripe fruit he saw, put its pulp on his heart, and uttered thanks for having lived another year.

A Seri girl began her harvesting career at the age of nine or ten, but she was forbidden to eat the first fruit she gathered, for if she did, she had "swallowed her arm" and would be a lazy picker forever. The Seri language has different terms for cactus harvesters who carry fruit or pulp in buckets (nowadays plastic), in their skirts, or strung on a flexible stick like small fish. Before plastic, Seri harvesters also might store their fruit in a bag made from a sea turtle's stomach.

The Seris manufactured some picking poles with spikes rather than hooks and made specialized types for the fruit of the saguaro, cardón, organ pipe, and pitahaya agria (*Stenocereus gummosus*, a cactus known to bear the most delicious fruit of all pitahayas). Preserved and portable, cactus fruit delicacies were as good as money in the bank. In fact, records from Pima and O'odham calendar sticks show that the cactus harvest could be dangerous, since the Apaches often raided at that time of year.

TRADITIONAL USES OF THE SAGUARO

RIBS

Harvesting sticks
  ("Cactus Puller")
  [Many groups]
Splints [Seri]
Calendar Sticks [Pima,
  Tohono O'odham]
Fence
Corral
Walls
Canes [Seri]
Shelves
Fire Drill [Pima]
Cradle Frame
Burden Basket Frame
  [Pima, Tohono O'odham]
Spindle [Pima]
Gambling Sticks [Pima,
  Tohono O'odham]
Birdcage
Bullroarer [Tohono O'odham]
Grave Covering
  [Tohono O'odham]
Oars
Ceremonial Objects [Pima,
  Tohono O'odham]

BOOTS

Water Container
Hunter's Carrying Container
  [Sobaipuri or Hohokam]
Doll Container [Seri]
Shroud [Hohokam]

FOOD

Fruit (raw)
Fruit (dehydrated)
Jam
Syrup
Wine [Seri, Apache, Yavapai,
  Maricopa, Tohono O'odham,
  Pima]
Vinegar
Meal
Bread
Candy
Pinole
Atole
Pudding
Oil

MISCELLANEOUS

Seeds used for chicken
  feed [Tohono O'odham]
Seeds used for tanning
Saguaro flesh used as poultice
  for pain [Seri]
Seed gruel used to increase
  milk supply in new mothers

The Cool of the Day / Early Summer Morning,
  "To My Mom & My Sister Imelda," *2000*
LEONARD F. CHANA

CELEBRATING THE HARVEST

Then came the rainmaking ceremony and the wine feasts, once widespread and still occasionally celebrated. Of these, the Tohono O'odham festival has been recorded in the richest detail. The *nawai't* or ceremony "to pull down the clouds" was the most important communal function in the Tohono O'odham traditional year. Several days of rituals were conducted by religious elders with titles such as the Keeper of the Smoke and He Who Desires Liquor. Diluted with water, saguaro syrup fermented in jars while dancers circled counterclockwise through the night. To bring on the fermentation and the summer rain, they sang songs about mountains, clouds, frogs, thunder, corn, and magic.

When the liquid turned to wine, it was time for the ceremony known as "sit and drink." In smooth, flowing language of great beauty, elders invoked the supernatural powers of rain and growth, centered in a deity who lived far away in spiritual "rainhouse" full of wind, water, and seeds. Between speeches came the actual drinking, until all the wine—highly perishable in 100°F summer heat—was gone. In ancient times no other alcohol existed, so the carnival was brief and sanctioned by society. (Young men supposedly colored the soles of their bare feet red to look attractive as they lay intoxicated on the ground.) But the religious experience was central: "The trance of drunkenness," wrote distinguished anthropologist Ruth Underhill, "is akin to the trance of vision."

Nevertheless, several calendar sticks record violence at wine feasts (although any event that rated a notch on a calendar stick must have been rare). When Hispanic and Anglo immigrants arrived, the sacred aspect of the ceremony was misunderstood. For that and other reasons, the practice declined, fading first among the Pimas. During the nineteenth and early twentieth centuries wine feasts were frequently outlawed, and now, although they are legal and even supported by the Roman Catholic Church, only a few Tohono O'odham villages still hold them.

Like wine from grapes, cactus wine results from the action of yeast on fruit sugar, which creates alcohol and carbon dioxide. All fermentation is somewhat unpredictable because complex organic processes can easily go wrong. Exposed to air and bacteria, alcohol turns into acetic acid and any wine to vinegar. Also like wine from grapes, cactus wines vary greatly.

Ruth Underhill described saguaro wine of the 1930s as a "thick dark-crimson liquor . . . brownish red . . . a gentle musty-tasting cider." Usually saguaro wines contain about as much alcohol as beer (perhaps 4 percent), so that large amounts must be swallowed to make someone "beautifully drunk [to] bring the rain and the clouds!" as the wine server says in the O'odham ceremony. Saguaro wine often acts as an emetic, but vomiting, according to

traditional belief, is good because it helps to bring rain. ("All I know is, that stuff gives me diarrhea," frankly added a modern Tohono O'odham elder.) The fruit of other columnar cacti also ferments, and until the Seris stopped making wine in the 1950s, they used organ pipe, cardón, and pitahaya agria fruit (which gave the strongest results).

The Seris produced a beer-like beverage from a blend of fruit and water, sometimes mixing it in a vat hollowed from a barrel cactus. They also made a more potent, long-lasting brew without added water, which sounds like the Arizona saguaro wine collected by the Smithsonian in the 1860s. After three years it had "improved with age," according to a government report, and was "in every respect superior to much of the wine on sale" in Washington. Blends may have been tried, too. Describing wine feasts among Piman groups in Sonora between 1756 and 1767, the missionary Ignaz Pfeffercorn said the drink was made from "pitahayas, tunas [prickly pear fruit], and maize." Apaches added herbs, corn, distilled alcohol and perhaps narcotic substances to their brew. But sometimes things went fatally wrong, for one Pima calendar stick mentions both accidental and deliberate poisoning of the wine.

PAYING RESPECT TO THE GIANT CACTUS

To the Seris, the cholla cactus, the cardón, and the saguaro were once people and are ancestors. Traditionally, to ensure a good life for a newborn Seri baby, the child's placenta was buried at the base of a saguaro or cardón, and while most Seris did not know their precise birthplaces, they did know where their placentas were buried. Later in life they might place green branches at the foot of the cactus to ask for good luck from its spirit.

In one Pima myth, an angry deity turns humans into saguaros. But in another story a grandmother chases two naughty runaway boys until they transform themselves into a saguaro and a palo verde tree. Motherless children, misbehavior, reverence for the saguaro, and the significance of the wine feast are recurring themes in Native American saguaro stories. "This vulnerable, childlike being must be treated well," the stories say, "or we will be the ones to suffer." Their tone suggests that respect for the giant cactus must be drilled into the young and the thoughtless. Rooted to the spot, the great human plant can neither fight back nor run away.

At a saguaro harvesting camp in the 1970s, the ethno-botanist Gary Paul Nabhan overheard a telling exchange when a young boy asked a matriarch if he could throw rocks to knock down the cactus fruit. Scandalized, she promptly scolded him: "NO! The saguaros—they are Indians too. You don't EVER throw ANYTHING at them. If you hit them in the head with rocks you could kill them. You don't ever stick anything sharp into their skin either, or they will just dry up and die. You don't do anything to hurt them. They are Indians."

Cactus carved by gunfire, Tucson, 1/27/90 MARK KLETT

A SERI SAGUARO STORY

One day, far away in Seri land, an old male mountain lion went on the prowl.

"I'm hungry!" he said.

Lean and mean and yellow-brown from the top of his rough round head to the twitching tip of his tail, he prowled across the desert at the edge of the sea. He prowled past stumpy, wrinkled elephant trees and tall, spiky boojums. He prowled through groves of giant green cactus: organ pipes, cardóns, senitas, and saguaros.

"I'm still hungry!" he growled.

Then the mountain lion came to a dark, deep cave. Inside the cave, four little cottontail rabbits were hiding.

The mountain lion pounced. ZAS! He caught one! And then he held the little rabbit down with his huge paw and took a look at it.

"Why, this cottontail has a yellow back!" he said. Like many cottontails, this one did indeed have a yellow streak in the fur along his spine. But this little rabbit was clever, and he was brave. He piped up, in a small trembling voice: "Yes! My back is yellow! My back is yellow—because—because—I like to kill old yellow mountain lions and carry them home to my cave on my back! The yellow rubs off!"

Then he called out to the other little rabbits, who were cowering in the darkest corner of the cave: "Bring out that old lion's head over there in the dark! I'll eat some of it, and then I'll go out and look for more lion tracks!"

And the other little rabbits rolled out a round, dry, yellow-brown saguaro boot from the back of the cave—crunch, crunch, crunch.

The mountain lion heard the raspy sound of the rolling saguaro boot. He saw the round, yellow-brown shape coming toward him through the dark of the cave.

"I'm not hungry any more!" he roared.

He let the first little rabbit go. And he ran away. Then the cottontails ran the opposite way and hid in a thorny thicket of mesquite trees. The first rabbit turned to the other little rabbits.

"From now on," he said, "wherever we go, you will go first, and I will take the safest place in the rear. Because I am the one who fooled the mean old mountain lion!"

Adapted from a Seri tale first recorded by Edward Moser and quoted in People of the Desert and Sea *by Richard Stephen Felger and Mary Beck Moser.*

A pair of saguaro boots PAUL ZIMMERMAN

Storm, *1997* DOUGLAS DENNISTON

"Saguaros are the most wonderful things in the world. When you're with saguaros, you're communicating with something profound and otherwise unattainable."
—Douglas Denniston

5

The Saguaro Harvest: Going Out with Stella

Before dawn on the last day of June, Stella Tucker sits in her saguaro camp and sips a cup of coffee. On the picnic table beside her sit a box of glazed doughnuts and a large jar of chiltepines, tiny dry peppers that score near the top of the tongue-on-fire scale.

"It's over," says Stella. She means the saguaro harvest of 2001. "The last two or three years the harvest has been real short," she explains.

This year unseasonable rains in the middle of June damaged the ripe fruit, so blackened empty husks surround the bases of the saguaros nearby. But we will trudge into the desert and try our luck anyway. A little may be left. In the distance a Gila woodpecker gives a sharp, aggressive cry, and the white wings of doves squeak as they come in for a landing. They're beating us to it.

"This was my grandmother's and my great aunt's saguaro camp," Stella says. "I love it here."

Stella Tucker's saguaro harvesting pole
W. ROSS HUMPHREYS

Her grandmother, Juana Ahill, first came to this spot by wagon, and earlier ancestors probably harvested fruit here from the ancestors of some of these saguaros, centuries before the place became part of Saguaro National Park and the road was paved. The camp includes an old-style ramada or *wa:tto* with a saguaro-rib roof, a semi-enclosed room tacked together from different building materials, and several outdoor cooking and eating areas. A flour-sack dish towel dangles from a clothesline, and the aroma of mesquite smoke hangs in the dawn air, which is still cool. To one side stand a water trailer, two Porta-Potties, and a Dumpster, all the property of "Saguaro Environmental Services." The fine dust underfoot is stamped with the prints of athletic shoes.

Behind Stella's head the sun pokes above the Tucson Mountains, giving a definite hint of heat to come. The first light reflects off the pads of prickly pear cacti, and they gleam like distant mirrors. Stella locates a pair of harvesting poles, both 15 to 20 feet long and constructed of two saguaro ribs attached end to end with baling wire. Wired crosswise near the thinnest end, each bears a creosote-wood cactus hook dyed red with saguaro juice. After protecting herself with a long-sleeved shirt and a sun visor, she leads the way to the fruit.

"Hook it from behind," she directs. "And catch! Well, you can't always catch. Some you can touch and they fall right down, but some are pretty attached to the saguaro. It's okay to have ants. If you've got ants or you've got rocks, just throw 'em in your pail."

The five-gallon bucket once contained stabilized chlorine tablets. Against its white plastic the blobs and splashes of cactus fruit look startlingly like blood.

"As long as there's a little bit of pink on the outside, you know it's ripe," Stella says. "They come in all different sizes. This one is small, but some are huge like a pear. See, this is what they look like when they fall to ground and dry up. See how it got shriveled up and dehydrated? You can keep it and then soak it in water and cook it later. Taste it!"

Raspberry fruit leather? Fig Newton cookie filling? The crunchy seeds add excellent contrast to the sticky candied pulp. Meanwhile Stella zeroes in on a promising stand of saguaros.

"Oh!" she says in disappointment. "Looks like the birds beat us to 'em."

A fallen saguaro lies nearby, its flesh half dry and half rotten, and beneath a creosote bush, nestled among shards of broken glass and an old leather shoe sole, a pincushion-sized *Carnegiea gigantea* is thriving.

"We used to come out in the middle of May," Stella recalls, shading her eyes to survey the neighboring saguaros. "I was late this year. I got here June the eighth."

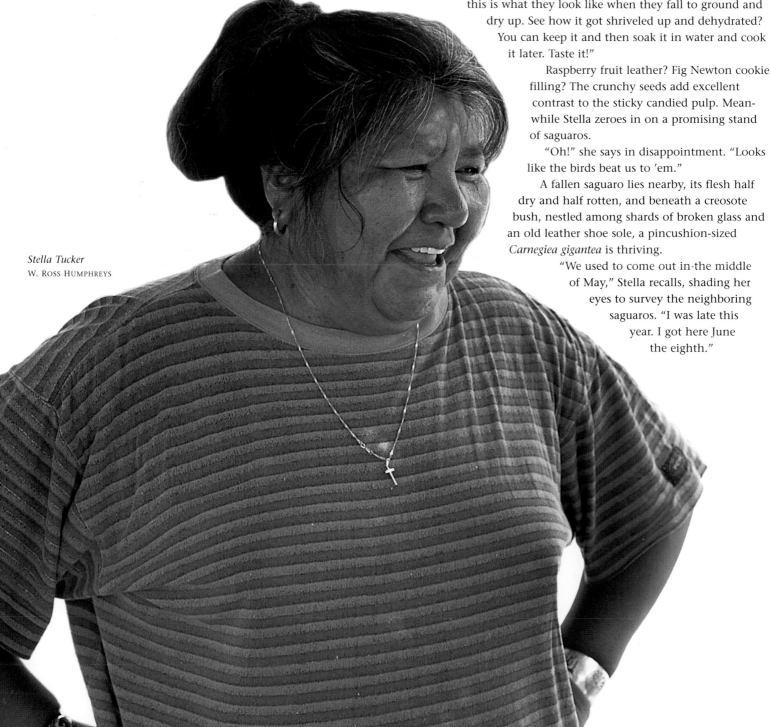

Stella Tucker
W. ROSS HUMPHREYS

Ripe saguaro fruit and seeds W. ROSS HUMPHREYS

The light grows brighter and the temperature has risen noticeably, probably into the eighties by now. Throughout the desert, cicadas are tuning up for a long hot day, and a small airplane drones overhead.

"We want to get all we can," says Stella, and she steps through a rusty barbed wire fence as a trio of doves flaps loudly away. "Some nice huge ones up here," she calls. "We gotta get 'em. Catcher—where's the catcher?"

The whole saguaro wiggles from the effort to detach a greenish fruit. The pole quivers, too, and Stella coaches from the sidelines: "You can really feel those muscles in your arms that you're using, can't you? Now, sometimes if you push *up* . . ." Thump! A fat egg-shaped fruit lands in the bucket. Another tug—a crisp rip—and then a dead plunk on the ground.

"Oops," says Stella.

The bucket is half full of colors: crimson, scarlet, vermilion, greenish pink, iceberg-lettuce white, scorched brown, rosy yellow. The seeds and ants are black.

"We can't reach up there." Stella, points out a 50-foot saguaro topped with plump pods. "Better let the birds have them."

At 7:45 we head back to camp, where Stella hangs her harvesting shirt in a palo verde tree, which also supports a thermometer, a hatchet, a dishcloth, a putty knife, a jar of cooking grease, a paper- and plastic-bag collection, a large hand-carved wooden spoon stained red, and the top section of a harvesting pole equipped with a 3-inch nail, Seri style. Stella sorts the dry fruit from the fresh and sets aside a collection of ruby-throated empty husks. "I like to keep these for decorations," she explains. "I put them on gifts." In years gone by, O'odham saguaro harvesters tossed a scraped husk back on the ground, red side up, because that way "it brings the rain."

The dehydrated fruit soaks while the fresh fruit is prepared. Traditionally cooks used a dry saguaro calyx or a fingernail to scrape about a teaspoon of pulp from each husk, but a Swiss Army knife helps to get every last drop.

"Don't waste," Stella says. "We don't waste. Only a quart of pulp from all that fruit. Isn't it amazing? Now mush the fruit with the water. Mush it up. Squish it. Use your hands. Now add the soaked fruit. Isn't it nice and slimy? Like mud, they say. So smooth!"

Now the lumpy red mixture goes tumbling into a blackened stew pot while she estimates that it will yield between one and two jars of syrup. Beneath a barbecue grill balanced on concrete blocks, a mesquite fire jumps up and licks the bottom of the pot.

"Pretty good," Stella allows. "We didn't get many rocks. See, the rocks go to the bottom and the ants come to the top. This is the first cooking, and then we strain it twice to separate the seeds and the fiber. We used to make jam."

Stella's 20-year-old daughter is not here to help this year because she's working for a computer firm in Baltimore. After half

Sun-dried saguaro fruit W. ROSS HUMPHREYS

Cooking down the fruit.

First straining through a screen.

Second straining through a flour sack.

Reducing the saguaro syrup.

Separating seeds from strained fiber.

an hour's simmering, stirring, and skimming, Stella pronounces the mixture ready to strain.

"See how the color changes?" she asks, and definitely the juice has lost its purple Beaujolais Nouveau tone and moved to a duller middle red, like boiling blood.

Two old gray saguaro ribs serve as handles for a square yard of window screen, which efficiently separates the steaming solids from the juice and then, suspended in the sun, becomes a seed-and-pulp dryer.

"This is my grandma Juana's strainer," Stella explains. "I don't want to get rid of it."

It works well. Next, the juice is forced through the flour sack from the clothesline, emerging a murkier, darker liquid that resembles hot red Kool-Aid.

"Make sure you squeeze the rag after you're done," Stella warns. "No wasting!"

It is nine o'clock in the morning, and the temperature is almost ninety degrees according to the thermometer in the palo verde tree. Stella adds more mesquite wood to the fire and pokes it with a stick so that steam quickly rises from the pot and the juice froths into orange foam. Within ten minutes it takes on a tomato-sauce color, but it does not smell like tomatoes at all.

When reduced to a slightly thickened consistency, which may take several hours, the saguaro syrup is done, and Stella serves it up. Surprise! Brilliant as paint, a burnt-sienna spoonful trickles over a scoop of vanilla ice cream, and frost, milk, fire, and cactus suddenly slam together. Yes, saguaro syrup does taste like molasses, but also like baked cherries spiked with chile, caramel, smoke, and perhaps a hint of tomato after all. There's a grassy note, too, which gives a distinctly vegetable edge. This is a flavor to be savored and discussed, a major memory like a fine Bordeaux. Left over from the sundaes, a few tablespoons of syrup glow in the sun at the bottom of an old artichoke-heart jar.

Stella looks around the camp thoughtfully. Bedrolls lie trussed in neat sausages on metal cots. The ground is scattered with palo verde pods, saguaro seeds, and pop tops from old-fashioned beer cans. Traffic hisses along the boundary of Saguaro National Park, and far away a dog is barking. "My grandma Juana had a stroke out here," she recalls, "and we took her to town."

By the end of a good harvest she has made gallons of syrup to take home with her. But this is a skimpy year.

"A lot of times," says Stella, "we get home and the elders are the only ones that really appreciate it. So we sell it to the elders. It's a dying tradition. Very few people do it now. There used to be quite a few families out here picking, but they've all died and their families don't continue."

Who will carry on?

"Hopefully," Stella says, "my daughter will. She knows the process. But it's hard work. It's *hot!*"

It is. By afternoon the temperature will surely soar above 100°F, with no rain in sight. Sweat and sunburn, cactus thorns, flies, fatigue, and dust would be the prevailing memories of the morning if others were not stronger— above all, that taste, big but not sweet, that lingers for the rest of the day.

Mouth full of saguaro. Desert blood.

SAGUARO FRUIT RECIPES

SAGUARO SYRUP (TRADITIONAL STYLE)

Saguaro fruit, ripe and dried
Water

Get up as early as possible. Harvest fruit with picking pole (kuipaD) and waterproof basket. Balance basket on head and carry back to camp.

Remove all inedible material from fruit. Reserve dried fruit to cook later. Break off dark, hardened calyx of saguaro flower and use as tool to split ripe fruit and scoop out pulp, or use fingernails. Collect pulp in large clay cooking pot (hi-to-ta-kut), cover with at least an equal amount of water, knead to mix thoroughly, and allow to soak until liquid is deep red (sometimes as long as a day, but the sooner the better, as it spoils quickly).

Boil deep-red mixture over a lively fire, stirring frequently with wooden ladle to extract sugar and flavor into water. When pulp comes to the top, strain contents of pot through special basket made of sotol (desert spoon) leaves, removing cactus fiber and seeds and reserving liquid. Spread pulpy material on mat in the sun to dry. Wash all sand and sediment from cooking pot and boil liquid again, skimming foam, until its darkened, reddish-brown color and slightly thickened texture show that it has reached desired concentration.

Hermetically seal in clean, narrow-necked clay jars (si-to-ta-kut), covering tops with potsherd cemented to jar with mud. This way the syrup, if not used for wine or other purposes, will keep as long as a year.

SAGUARO SYRUP (MODERN STYLE)

Saguaro fruit, ripe and dried
Water

Get up as early as possible. Harvest fruit with a picking pole and plastic buckets. Back at camp, remove all inedible materials from fruit and reserve dried fruit in plastic bag to cook later. Scoop pulp from ripe fruit with small knife and collect in bucket.

Cover pulp with water, knead to mix thoroughly, and allow to soak until the liquid is deep red, at least 30 minutes and maybe longer (under refrigeration this time can be extended safely to a day). Transfer to 4-gallon enamelware cooking pot and boil, stirring frequently, over lively fire (or medium heat on stove) for about 30 minutes to extract sugar and flavor. When pulp rises to top, strain mixture first through window-screen mesh to remove pulp and seeds, then through flour sack to remove fine sediment. Reserve liquid. Spread pulpy material on window screen in the sun to dry. Reserve for another use.

Return liquid to clean pot and boil, skimming foam, for at least 30 minutes and up to several hours, until a darkened, reddish-brown color and slightly thickened texture show that it has reached the desired concentration. Seal in clean recycled glass jars, such as pickle jars or baby-food jars. Refrigerate for long-term storage.

SAGUARO SUNDAE

Ripe saguaro fruit
1/3 cup orange liqueur, optional
1 tablespoon vanilla extract
1 quart vanilla ice cream

Scoop pulp from fruit with knife or spoon and freeze until needed. Before serving time, thaw 1 pint pulp and flavor with liqueur, if using, and vanilla extract. Spoon over ice cream. Serves 4.

(Adapted from Sandal English, Fruits of the Desert, p. 33)

SAGUARO SUNDAE II

Saguaro syrup (see above)
Vanilla ice cream

Spoon 2 to 3 tablespoons syrup over each serving of ice cream.

Copper souvenir spoon, c. 1950,
courtesy Ron and Marcia Spark
W. ROSS HUMPHREYS

6
Saguaros and Modern Culture

S aguaro you today?" asks a bumper sticker on the rump of a car, and a little grinning cactus figure zooms away through Arizona traffic.

Did corporate America kidnap the saguaro, as journalist Lawrence Cheek has suggested? "We have always needed icons to represent and explain the West," he theorized. Certainly the giant cactus icon is part of the myth of the West, where fact and fiction have always gone hand in hand.

In 1854 John Russell Bartlett set out to give "a full and correct description of this extraordinary production of the vegetable kingdom." His *Personal Narrative* remains a trove of saguaro lore and an emotional homage to "our friend the *petahaya*." Bartlett was a frontier cactophiliac, to borrow

Farmer John meat-packing plant mural by Leslie Grimes and Arno Jordan, Tucson, Arizona
W. ROSS HUMPHREYS

(top) Saguaro bathing beauty, (bottom) cactus football player, 1941
TUCSON SUNSHINE CLIMATE CLUB

Gary Nabhan's humorous term for cactus lovers. Next to "the graceful *petahaya*," Bartlett disdained other desert plants as "dwarfish."

"The great cereus," he wrote, "raises its lofty head above all other plants, attaining its greatest perfection in this barren and desolate place." Fantasy added glitter to reality: "If one unused to these remarkable plants should suddenly be brought to this place," and if he saw a cactus forest "as we did by moonlight," he would "imagine himself in the midst of the ruins of a magnificent palace, the columns of which were alone left standing."

Fifty years later, a similar thought struck John Van Dyke. "On the mountains and the mesas the sahuaro is so common that perhaps we overlook its beauty of form," he wrote. "Yet its lines are as sinuous as those of a Moslem minaret, its flutings as perfect as those of a Doric column."

Writing in 1932, Homer Shantz drew a more logical comparison: "The Cactus Forest ranks with the great Redwoods, not in age and not in mass of vegetation, but certainly in unique character, and surpasses them in variety of form." A botany professor who became president of the University of Arizona, Shantz was largely responsible for the creation of Saguaro National Monument the following year. "Nowhere in the world is there so fine a stand of the giant saguaro," Shantz said. He was ahead of his time in insisting that this remarkable area "must be protected or it will soon be destroyed."

As the twentieth century progressed, many voices continued to call for the preservation of the saguaro in a quickly urbanizing West. *Carnegiea gigantea* has become a symbol of wilderness and a rallying point for conservationists. The great cactus now tends to stand for Nature being destroyed by Man. The frontier is gone, and in the myth of the modern West, the saguaro is the good guy. It wears the white hat.

Some have found spiritual meaning in the giant cactus. To poet Richard Shelton, saguaros are "the comic gods of the desert, gods whose comedy can be quickly turned to tragedy by disease or man's casual brutality." To Steve Richard, a research geologist for the Arizona Geological Survey, saguaros send a different kind of signal.

"In most cases, when you start seeing saguaros around, you know you don't have to go very much farther to find bedrock," he said. "I use them when I'm mapping because the distribution of cactus coincides with the rocks."

For some visitors, the pure strangeness of saguaros turns the desert into a plant zoo or a succulent sideshow. Saguaros seem destined to become tacky postcards, and over the years many visitors to the desert have succumbed to the urge to be photographed with the local monsters, even sometimes daringly perched in their spiny arms. (Of course, this is also a way to relate to them.) In the 1940s, members of the Tucson Sunshine Climate Club promoted the booming desert city by costuming models in scanty outfits (including a bathing suit made of real prickly pear topped off with real saguaro) and posing them for publicity photos in the desert. Among many "saguaro girls," they photographed one "saguaro boy" who modeled a genuine cactus football helmet.

Meanwhile, more serious people were trying to save the giant cactus from what they feared was imminent extinction. Throughout the famous forest, saguaros by

Western archetypes abound in Evening in the Foothills, *1940*
DALE NICHOLS

the thousands were falling ill and dying. Naturalist Paul Griswold Howes described the gruesome scene in 1954: "The giants may be found rotting and sloughing away, their beautiful green bodies gradually fading into masses of black fetid paste which slips to the ground, there to become a horrid broth infested with maggots and beetles and other insects."

Saguaros, like any other living things, are susceptible to disease. By the 1940s, scientists had noticed that when one of the plants is injured, it "bleeds" a thick, sludgy substance, first brown and then black, the cause of which was determined to be several groups of *Erwinia cacticida* bacteria, carried by moth larvae. Many of the sick cacti were bulldozed into large pits in an effort to contain the disease, and some saguaros were even dosed with the newest wonder drug, penicillin. Nothing seemed to help. Respected plant pathologists predicted that saguaros would vanish from Saguaro National Monument by the year 2000, which speeded the establishment of the western unit of the monument in 1961.

"If the great saguaros should eventually disappear, it would be a tragedy," Howes lamented. "The saguaros symbolize the pioneer spirit. . . . They have a right to survive and they have a supreme claim upon the strange habitat which they won so valiantly and which they now deservedly dominate."

This is an example of what Steenbergh and Lowe deplored as the myth of the "dying hero." Prophecies of gloom and doom actually began as early as 1902 and keep on coming. As recently as the 1990s another false rumor made the rounds, claiming that the giant cactus had been attacked by a fatal condition called "brown decline."

Sympathy for the saguaro recently led a third-grade class at Teaticket Elementary School in Falmouth, Massachusetts, to sell their outgrown clothes and toys to raise money to support the plants at Saguaro National Park.

"They sent us $143 to help the cactus," recalled Park Ranger Melanie Florez, smiling. After careful consideration, the park staff used the funds for the children's educational program.

If they had Mark Twain's way with words, saguaros might say the reports of their extinction have been greatly exaggerated. Saguaros die in public, so to speak, and usually quite slowly and pathetically. But nature is never simple. According to studies done by Steenbergh and Lowe, and confirmed by others, the much-vaunted plague of the Fifties was probably just part of a natural progression— a way to dispose of cacti that had already been damaged fatally by catastrophic freezes.

However, censuses taken in Saguaro National Monument at midcentury also revealed a shortage of young saguaros. Was it caused by nurse-plant decimation due to livestock grazing and woodcutting (now banned)? Was it caused by rodents, flicker nests, disease, climate, or the theft of young plants? Most likely the true cause was a combination of these factors, with climate a prime suspect. Despite the panic over fading populations of saguaros, plant ecologist Raymond Turner explained it as essentially connected to climatic conditions.

"We basically have been enjoying dense saguaro forests that are a legacy of conditions one hundred years ago," he said. "Conditions are different now." In order to study those conditions, Turner examined the long-term records of July and August rainfall for the Tucson area, which show that the rain in those two months has generally contributed about 40 percent of the annual total. Next, he and other scientists looked to see when the July and August rainfall exceeded 70 percent of the annual total, an arbitrary extreme. Prior to 1890, that occurred about every third year. Since then, however, it has only happened every eleventh year on the average. The decline in July-August rainfall alone would explain the drop in numbers of new saguaros, given the short-lived seeds and seedlings with such precise moisture requirements.

Long-term studies have revealed no urgent cause for alarm about the future of the species. The 2000 census shows a 125-percent increase in juvenile saguaros over the 1990 count. "The census showed many more juveniles than ten years ago, due to the correct weather conditions," said park plant specialist Mark Holden. "This pulse of juveniles is part of the whole saguaro life cycle." Saguaros are by no means racing down the road to endangerment or extinction either in the United States or in Mexico.

Mark Dimmitt, director of natural history at the Arizona-Sonora Desert Museum, says that fear about their

Sonoran Desert hiker DAVID H. SMITH

Treating saguaro with penicillin,
c. 1950s PHOTOGRAPHER UNKNOWN

future is one of the most potent misconceptions people have about saguaros. "The story has been propagated that there is an unsuspected, unmitigated natural disaster, when actually they are doing quite well as a species," he commented. "We are concerned about general habitat loss for certain ones near cities, but as a whole, they are doing well."

THE THREAT OF FIRE

Some threats are very real. "Saguaros are really susceptible to wildfires," said Holden, "and those fires are caused by encroachment of exotic grasses." Grasses not native to the desert encourage fires and help them to spread more quickly. "Fires are not part of the natural cycle of the desert," said Florez soberly, recounting stories of disastrous blazes at the park. Not only do the fires kill and damage saguaros, but they also kill desert tortoises and other animal and plant residents that are unable to escape.

Fires may be set by human beings, who constitute the biggest single influence on the future of the saguaro besides climate. The 2000 census indicates that the total number of saguaros in the Tucson Basin is at least a million, so they still outnumber human beings in the area, though the gap is closing. Explosive population growth in the Sonoran Desert, both in Arizona and northern Mexico, has changed the environment more drastically than any factor since the last major climate shift. Meanwhile the relationship between saguaros and people continues to evolve.

PLAYING WITH CLICHÉ

Cartoonists love saguaros; serious artists find them challenging. The goal of Tucson landscape photographer Bill Lesch is "to play with cliché." He has a particular interest in dead saguaros. "I love the way they decompose, their skeletal positions, the bleached bones. Then it's like a drawing—you see them a different way. And I've done some close-up shots of saguaro skin on the ground. Like pottery or ceramic, cactus skin folds up in different ways."

Douglas Denniston has studied the Sonoran Desert throughout his long career as a painter. Just outside his studio window stands a slender 9-foot saguaro, still armless, that he rescued from a construction site more than thirty years ago, when it was small enough to fit in the trunk of his car.

"What I like about saguaros is their variety," he says. "And the variety is, as it is in human beings, infinite. Saguaros always have great presence. They can elevate, so they can occupy a space in a painting that isn't possible with a tree. There's infinite variety also in their grouping, and they can be any number of colors. And the size is wonderful! Not so big that you can't understand it all, but big enough to be imposing."

Blue Saguaro and Jupiter WILLIAM LESCH

Like many Sonoran Desert residents, "I have a favorite saguaro," confided Ranger Florez. Yet even among card-carrying desert rats there are holdouts, including the nature writer Joseph Wood Krutch, who was lukewarm about saguaros. "These monsters are almost the trademark of Arizona," he noted in *The Desert Year*, but he complained that the state flower was "a little inadequate for so gigantic a plant." Personally, he preferred ocotillos. Ever crusty, Edward Abbey wrote, "Compared to the saguaro, the cardón is a crude hulking brute of an organism. I'll take the cardón."

But it seems unlikely that any other desert plant will ever become a superhero in a comic book. In *Saguarrior* (published by LoS CoMICS in 1997), the gentle veterinarian Dr. Arthur Wolfe sets off on a peaceful drive through the desert and finds himself suddenly ("YEOOOOW!") transformed. ("UNGHHH!")

"WHAT THAA . . ." he cries. "GREEN SKIN! STICKERS?? HAVE I BECOME A CACTUS??!!!"

Yes! He has! And on the next page he's exercising his super powers, which include ("FFFFZZZUU!!!") projectile spines. His cactus counterpart stars in another comic by the same artists, which begins

There is a land that's rough and dry
Which lies beneath the western sky
Living here can at times be tricky
You won't find Barney, Bart or Mickey
But from this desert here comes . . . STICKY.

A youthful rebel, this comic "anti-cactus" plays in a rock band called Sticky and the Deserters.

On the other hand, Douglas Denniston takes a melancholy view of the future of the saguaro in the

Saguaros make excellent neighbors. When Jim and Loma Griffith moved into their westside Tucson home in 1973, the front yard was already occupied by a colony of young saguaro cacti transplanted in the 1940s by the previous owner. Now the quiet green giants have matured, and the second saguaro generation is taking root. "There are eight babies outside my study window," Griffith reports.

TRICIA McINROY/TUCSON CITIZEN

Saguaro as superhero
LoS COMICS

new urban West. "I can't conceive of any happy relation between rampant development and saguaros," he said. "There's probably nothing worse than seeing a bulldozer knock down a big saguaro. That is just awful. And there's nothing more pathetic than a saguaro on a golf course."

Nothing illustrates the complex, tragicomic relationship between people and saguaros better than a story that begins with a small newspaper article published on February 6, 1982:

PHOENIX, AZ (AP)—A 27-year-old Phoenix man was killed when a saguaro cactus he shot fell on him, authorities said.

Maricopa County sheriff's deputies said David M. Grundman fired a shotgun at least two times at a 27-foot cactus.

The shots caused a 23-foot section of the cactus to fall and crush Grundman, deputies said.

Deputies said Grundman already had felled one saguaro.

Destruction of cacti is a misdemeanor under Arizona law.

Grundman and a friend were in a desert area north of here when the incident occurred Thursday afternoon, deputies said.

Reprinted with permission of The Associated Press.

Cactophiliacs everywhere cheered for the saguaro. Not long after, the Austin Lounge Lizards, a Texas band, paid tribute to the martyred cactus in a rollicking ballad called "Saguaro." Featured on their album *Creatures from the Black Saloon* (1984), it celebrates the epic battle between "twenty-seven feet of succulent" and "a noxious little twerp" who "saw the giant plants as the Clanton gang/ and himself as Wyatt Earp."

What does the future hold for us all? Perhaps there are better survival strategies than brains can imagine. Certainly global warming, if it creates more and bigger deserts, will favor saguaros in their march through North America, which is moving at a gallop, botanically speaking. "The cacti in general and the saguaro in particular are among the relative newcomers to the plant kingdom," said Steenbergh and Lowe. If they continue quickly evolving to survive cold, who knows where saguaros will go?

Perhaps we should pay close attention to the theory that flowering plants, by enticing us to eat and grow them—and to admire and sympathize with them—are using us for their own ends rather than the other way around. Giant cacti may do their work so slowly that we simply don't detect it. At any rate, the story of saguaros is clearly far from over, as Chip Littlefield, another ranger at Saguaro National Park, recently observed. "Saguaros are still outliving their researchers," he said.

ACKNOWLEDGMENTS

Many thanks to all the people who shared their knowledge, experience, and art to make this book possible, especially Ray Turner, who reviewed the text for scientific accuracy. Any remaining errors are ours. At Saguaro National Park we wish to thank Meg Weesner, Melanie Florez, Tom Danton, Richard Hill, Mark Holden, and Chip Littlefield. Also generous with their expertise were Stella Tucker, Bunny Fontana, Jonathan Mabry, Sue Wells, Doug Denniston, Mark Dimmitt, Jim Griffith, Dale Turner, David Burckhalter, Bill Lesch, David Yetman, Gary Gaynor, P. K. Weis, Deborah Shelton, and Riva Dean. Special thanks also go to Ron and Marcia Spark, Peter and Dana Booth, Ofelia Zepeda, Meg Quinn, R. R. Knudson, Paul Hackwell, The Rosewood Corporation and Paul Mirocha.

ILLUSTRATION CREDITS

Arizona Historical Society: 53
Russ Bishop: 17 (center)
David Burckhalter: 2 (top)
Tony Celentano: 32
Leonard Chana: 37 acrylic on canvas, 14¾ x 30 in., courtesy Dana & Peter Booth
Carr Clifton: ii-iii, 14, 20-21
Edward S. Curtis: 33 Library of Congress-USZ62-101181
Douglas Denniston: 40-41 *Storm* 1997, oil on linen, 52 x 52 in., courtesy the artist
Jack Dykinga: front cover, inside front cover-title page, 5, 30-31, 58
George Engelmann: 6 (bottom) and 10 (top) from "Cactaceae of the Boundary." In *Report on the United States and Mexican Boundary Survey*, edited by William H. Emory, courtesy Bernard L. Fontana
Jim Honcoop: 16 (left), 17 (left)
George H.H. Huey: 30 (left inset), 31 (right inset), 60-inside back cover
W. Ross Humphreys: 2 (bottom), 10 (bottom), 11, 27, 35 (bottom), 42-49
Stephen Ingram: 18-19
Kerrick James: 13, 29
Mark Klett: 4, 39
William Lesch: 54-55

LoS CoMICS: 56
Jonathan Mabry: 35 (top)
Tricia McInroy/Tucson *Citizen*: 56-57
Paul Mirocha: 24, 26-28 (illustrations)
Balduin Möllhausen: 3 *Cereus giganteus on Bill Williams Fork*, 1858, from *Diary of a Journey from the Mississippi to the Coasts of the Pacific*, vol. 2, courtesy Arizona Historical Society
Dale Nichols: 51 *Evening In the Foothills*, 1940, oil on canvas, 25¼ x 22 in., collection of the Tucson Museum of Art. 1992.398
Henry Cheever Pratt: 6-7 *View from Maricopa Mountain Near the Rio Gila*, 1855, oil on canvas, 33 x 48 in. unframed, courtesy The Rosewood Corporation, Dallas, Texas
Randy Prentice: 8, 22-23, 25, 26, 30 (right inset)
Meg Quinn: 16 (right), 17 (right)
David H. Smith: 52
Godfrey Sykes: 1 courtesy Arizona Historical Society
Tucson Sunshine Climate Club: 50 (both) courtesy Arizona Historical Society
Tom Vezo: 9, 12, 15, 24, 28
Thomas Wiewandt: 31 (left inset)
James S. Wood/*Arizona Daily Star*: 34
Paul Zimmerman: 42 (bottom)

SOURCES

Abbey, Edward. *Cactus Country*. New York: Time-Life Books, 1973.

———. *Desert Solitaire*. New York: McGraw-Hill, 1968.

Bartlett, John Russell. *Personal Narrative of Explorations and Incidents in Texas, New Mexico, California, Sonora, and Chihuahua*. New York: Appleton, 1854.

Benson, Lyman. *The Cacti of Arizona*. Tucson, Ariz.: University of Arizona Press, 1969.

Bowers, Janice E. "Catastrophic Freezes in the Sonoran Desert." *Desert Plants* 2 (Spring, 1980): 232-236.

Britton, N. L., and J. N. Rose. *The Cactaceae*. Vol. 1-4. Washington, D.C.: Carnegie Institution, 1920.

Crosswhite, Frank S. "The Annual Saguaro Harvest and Crop Cycle of the Papago, with Reference to Ecology and Symbolism." *Desert Plants* 2 (Spring 1980): 3-62.

Engelmann, George. "Cactaceae of the Boundary." In *Report on the United States and Mexican Boundary Survey*, edited by William H. Emory. 3 Vol. Washington, D.C.: 1857.

English, Sandal. *Fruits of the Desert*. Tucson, Ariz.: Arizona Daily Star, 1981.

Felger, Richard Stephen, and Mary Beck Moser. *People of the Desert and Sea*. Tucson, Ariz.: University of Arizona Press, 1985.

Fontana, Bernard L. "Ethnobotany of the Saguaro, an Annotated Bibliography." *Desert Plants* 2 (Spring 1980): 63-78.

Hazen-Hammond, Susan. "The Storyteller's Tale: A Legend of the Tohono O'odham." *Arizona Highways* 75 (April 1999): 41-43.

Hollis Bravo, Helia and Léia Scheinvar. *El interestante mundo de las cactáceas*. Mexico City: Fondo de Cultura Económica, 1995.

Howes, Paul Griswold. *The Giant Cactus Forest and Its World*. Boston: Little, Brown, 1954.

Krutch, Joseph Wood. *The Desert Year*. New York: Sloan, 1952.

Lumholtz, Carl. *New Trails in Mexico*. New York: Scribner, 1912.

Nabhan, Gary Paul. *The Desert Smells Like Rain*. San Francisco, Calif.: North Point Press, 1982.

Niethammer, Carolyn. *American Indian Food and Lore*. New York: Collier, 1974.

Phillips, Steven J., and Patricia Wentworth Comus, eds. *A Natural History of the Sonoran Desert*. Tucson, Ariz., and Berkeley, Calif.: Arizona-Sonora Desert Museum Press and University of California Press, 2000.

Russell, Frank. "The Pima Indians." In *Twenty-Sixth Annual Report of the Bureau of American Ethnology*. Washington, D.C.: Government Printing Office, 1908.

Saxton, Dean and Lucille Saxton. *O'othham hoho'ok a'agitha: Legends and Lore of the Pima and Papago Indians*. Tucson, Ariz.: University of Arizona Press, 1973.

Shantz, Homer L. "The Saguaro Forest." *National Geographic Magazine* 71 (April 1937): 515-532.

Shelton, Richard. *Going Back to Bisbee*. Tucson, Ariz.: University of Arizona Press, 1992.

Spaulding, Effie Southworth. "Mechanical Adjustment of the Suaharo (*Cereus giganteus*) to Varying Quantities of Stored Water." *Bulletin of the Torrey Botanical Club* 32 (February 1905): 57-68.

Steenbergh, Warren F., and Charles Lowe. *Ecology of the Saguaro: I*. Washington, D.C.: National Park Service, 1976.

———. *Ecology of the Saguaro: II*. Washington, D.C.: National Park Service, 1977.

———. *Ecology of the Saguaro: III*. Washington, D.C.: National Park Service, 1983.

Swenson, May. *May Out West: Poems of May Swenson*. Logan, Utah: Utah State University Press, 1996.

Turner, Raymond M., Janice E. Bowers, and Tony L. Burgess. *Sonoran Desert Plants: An Ecological Atlas*. Rev. ed. Tucson, Ariz.: University of Arizona Press, 1995.

Underhill, Ruth. *Papago Indian Religion*. New York: Columbia University Press, 1946.

———. *People of the Crimson Evening*. Washington, D.C.: U.S. Indian Service, 1951.

———. *Singing for Power*. Berkeley, Calif.: University of California Press, 1938.

Van Dyke, John C. *The Desert*. New York: Scribner, 1901.

Wright, Harold Bell. *Long Ago Told*. New York: Appleton, 1929.

Saguaros on desert bajada, Sand Tank Mountains, Barry M. Goldwater Range, Arizona JACK DYKINGA

Tonto National Forest and Roosevelt Lake GEORGE H. H. HUEY